Giant
Book of
Card Games

♠ ♣ ♦ ♥

Sheila Anne Barry
Alfred Sheinwold
&
William A. Moss

Sterling Publishing Company, Inc.
New York

10 9 8 7 6 5 4 3 2 1

Published In 1998 by Sterling Publishing Company, Inc.
387 Park Avenue South, New york. N.Y. 10016

Material in this collection was adapted from
101 Best Family Card Games © Alfred Sheinwold
10-Minute Card Games © William A. Moss
World's Best Card Games For One © Sheila Anne Barry

Distributed in Canada by Sterling Publishing
c/o Canadian Manda Group
One Atlantic Avenue, Suite 105
Toronto, Ontario, Canada M6K 3E7

Distributed in Great Britain and Europe by Chris Lloyd
463 Ashley Road, Parkstone, Poole,
Dorset, BH14 0AX, United Kingdom

Distibuted in Australia by Capricorn Link (Australia) Pty Ltd.
P.O. Box 6651, Baulkham Hills, Business Centre
NSW 2153, Australia

Sterling ISBN 0-8069-4809-4

Contents

SECTION 1
Family Games

Why Family Card Games?

My own experience makes me feel that every family will benefit from playing card games together.

It is, first of all, fun—and a splendid way to enjoy spending time in each other's company. It's also a great way to get to learn how each other's mind works, which can be important to both parent and child.

Then, too, it's a healthy experience for a child to play with grownups as an equal. It adds to a child's self-esteem when he or she feels included and part of the fun— to say nothing of the implied supposition that the child is intelligent enough to learn the games and worthy of playing them with experienced competitors.

Another major benefit is that the child gets practice in losing without squawking and winning without crowing. (Many adults could use some of this practice, too!)

A young child also can learn about numbers and easy arithmetic from card games. And people of any age can exercise their brain by the logical thinking needed in the more advanced games.

—Alfred Sheinwold

1

For the Family with Very Young Children

These games are for children who are too young to think—and for grownups who would rather *not* think! Sometimes it's hard to tell whether the children or the grownups laugh harder!

Pig

This is a very hilarious game for children or for adults to play with children. Anybody can learn it in two or three minutes, and one extra minute makes you an expert!

Players: 3 to 13—5 or 6 make the best game.

Cards: 4 of a kind for each player in the game.
For example, 5 players would use 20 cards:
4 Aces, 4 Kings, 4 Queens, 4 Jacks, and 4 10s.
For 6 players you would add the 9s.

The Deal: Any player shuffles and deals four cards to each player.

To Win the Game: Get four of a kind in your own hand, or be quick to notice it when somebody else gets four of a kind.

The Play: The players look at their cards to see if they were dealt four of a kind. If nobody has four of a kind, each player puts some unwanted card *face down* on the table and passes it to the player to the left, receiving a card at the same time from the player to the right.

If, still, nobody has four of a kind, each player once again passes a card to the left and gets a new card from the right.

The play continues in this way until one player gets four of a kind. That player stops passing or receiving cards. Instead, he puts his finger to his nose.

The other players must be quick to notice this, and each of them must stop passing in order to put a finger to his nose. The last player to put a finger to his nose is the *Pig*.

Strategy: In trying to put together four of a kind, you usually start with a pair. For example, suppose you are dealt two Kings, one Queen, and one Ace. Keep the two Kings, and pass either the Queen or the Ace. As soon as you get another King, save all three of them, and pass your fourth card. Sooner or later your fourth King will come in.

Don't get so interested in looking for your own four of a kind that you are blind to what the other players are doing. Keep one eye on everybody else, particularly on those who look very eagerly at the cards they are receiving. The eager player probably has three of a kind and is just waitng for the fourth.

The best *Pig* player I know is a seven-year old girl who doesn't try very hard to make four of a kind. She always tries to look excited, and talks and squeals as she gets each card, just as though she had three of a kind. While doing all of this, she watches the other players to see which of them are most interested in her and which are interested in their own hands.

She knows that the players who are interested in *her* have *bad* hands, but that those who are thinking about the *game* have *good* hands. So little Lisa knows which players to watch, and she is never caught!

Donkey

This is the same game as *Pig*, except that when you get four of a kind you put your hand face down on the table quietly instead of putting your finger to your nose. You still get a card from your right, but you just pass it along to the left, leaving your four of a kind untouched on the table.

As the other players see what has happened, they likewise put their cards down quietly. The idea is to keep up the passing and the conversation while some player plays on without realizing that the hand has really ended.

If you're the last player to put your cards on the table, you lose the hand. This makes you a D. The next time you lose, you become a D-O. The third time you become a D-O-N. This keeps on, until finally you become a D-O-N-K-E-Y.

The D-O-N-K-E-Y loses the game, and the winner is the player who has the smallest number of letters.

Donkey Buttons

Equipment: **Buttons—one less than there are players.**

This is the same game as *Donkey*, except that when you get four of a kind, you shout, "Donkey!" and quickly grab a button from the middle of the table. There is one button less than there are players, so the last player to grab doesn't get a button—and becomes a D. The game continues in this way until somebody becomes a D-O-N-K-E-Y.

At the end of the game, the D-O-N-K-E-Y has to bray "*heehaw*" three times.

10

My Ship Sails

Players: 4 to 7—4 or 5 make the best game.

Cards: 7 for each player.

The Deal: Any player shuffles and deals seven cards to each player.

To Win the Game: Get seven cards of the same suit.

The Play: Each player looks at his hand and passes one card to the left, receiving at the same time one card from the right. The play goes on in the same way as in *Pig* or *Donkey*. The only difference is that you are trying to collect cards that are all of the same suit.

There are many different ways of ending a hand. When you get seven cards of the same suit, you put your cards down immediately and say, "My ship sails!" Another way is to say nothing but to put your finger to your nose as in *Pig*.

If it takes too long to finish a hand, try one of the shorter games—*My Bee Buzzes* or *My Star Twinkle*s (page 12).

Strategy: Begin by trying to collect the suit that you have most of. For example, if you have four or five hearts, pass the other cards and try to collect more hearts.

You may run into trouble if some other player tries to collect the same suit that you are collecting. To guard against this, start collecting a second suit if you don't have any luck with the first. If you can get three cards in a second suit, you can then start to pass the cards of your first suit and switch your plan.

For example, suppose you start with three hearts, two spades, one club, and one diamond. Keep passing the clubs and diamonds until you get another heart or another spade. If you get one more—or a third spade before any heart is passed to you, you may suspect that somebody else is saving the hearts. Your best bet is to break up your hearts and to try to get seven spades instead.

If you have four or more cards in the same suit, it doesn't pay to break. Sit tight and hope that one of the other players will break first and pass the cards that you need.

My Star Twinkles

This is the same as *My Ship Sails* except that you need only five cards of the same suit (and two odd cards) to win a hand. In this game it takes only two or three minutes to play a hand.

My Bee Buzzes

This is the same as *My Ship Sails* except that you need only six cards of the same suit to end the hand. Each player gets seven cards, but needs only six cards in the same suit (and one odd card) to win the hand. It takes less time to finish a hand in this game than in *My Ship Sails*.

Through the Window

Players: 3 to 13—the more the merrier.

Cards: 4 to each player.

The Deal: The dealer shuffles and deals four cards to each player.

To Win the Game: Win the most cards.

The Play: The dealer begins by saying, "I looked through the window and saw . . . ." Just at this moment, and not before, he turns up one of his four cards so that all the players can see it.

Then, each player (including the dealer) must try to say an animal or thing beginning with the same letter of the alphabet as the card that has been turned up. For example, if the card is an Ace, you might call out "Ant," "Alligator," "Alaska," or anything else that begins with the letter A. If the card is a Nine, you might call out "Nachos" or "Nut."

The first player to call out a correct word takes the card and starts his pile of captured cards separate from the four cards that were dealt to him. Then the person to the left of the dealer says, "I looked through the window and saw . . . ," turning up one of her cards. The game continues in the same way, in turn to the left, until all the cards originally dealt have been turned up and captured. Each person keeps his own pile of captured cards, and the one who captures the most wins the game. The captured cards have nothing to do with each player's original four cards, since each player had exactly four chances to turn up a card.

As soon as a word has been used to win a card, no player can use that same word again. For example, if you have used the word "Stone" to capture a Seven, neither you nor any other player can use the word "Stone" to capture any other card beginning with an S.

Concentration

Players: Any number at all—the more the merrier.

Cards: 1 pack.

The Deal: Spread the cards face down on a table. Don't bother to put them down neatly, but just jumble them up, making sure that no two cards overlap.

To Win the Game: Capture the largest number of cards.

The Play: Before play begins, the players should be told what their turn is, so that they know whether they are first, second, third, and so on.

The first player turns up any card and then turns up any other card. If the two cards match (for example, if they are two Aces or two Kings), the first player captures them as her pair. She then has another turn and proceeds to turn up two more cards in the hope of finding a pair. When she turns up two cards that are not a pair, she must turn them face down again in the same position. It now becomes the turn of the next player.

Strategy: The trick is to remember the cards that have been turned up and exactly where on the table they are. For example, suppose a player turns up a King and a 10. He had to turn those cards face down again. You do your best to remember exactly where that King is and where that 10 is. Then, when it is your turn, you turn up a card on an entirely different part of the table, hoping to find another King or another 10. If you find another King, you can go right to the first King like a homing pigeon and you'll have a pair of Kings to capture. If you find another 10, you can go right to the first 10 and capture those cards, too.

If you try to remember too many cards, you may forget them all. It is much better to begin by trying to remember only two or three cards. When you find that you can do that easily, try remembering four cards. In this way you can gradually increase your skill until you can accurately remember the whereabouts of seven or eight cards at a time. This should be enough to win almost any game.

Tossing Cards into a Hat

Players: Any number, but the game is best with two or three.

Cards: 1 old deck—or 2 old decks if playing with more than 3 people.

Equipment: An old felt or straw hat. A sheet of newspaper.

The Deal: Divide the cards equally among the players.

To Win the Game: Toss the largest number of cards into the hat.

The Play: Place the hat on a sheet of newspaper at the other end of the room, with crown down and brim up.

Standing the whole length of the room away from the hat, each player in turn flips one card towards the hat, with the object of landing the card inside the hat.

Each player keeps track of the cards he has landed inside the hat. If a card lands on the brim, it counts as only one-half a point. If a card on the brim of the hat is knocked in by any player, it counts a full point for the player who originally threw it.

Strategy: The trick is to hold the card between your thumb and fore-finger with your wrist bent inwards towards your body. If you then straighten out your wrist suddenly with a flick and release the card at the same time, you can make it sail all the way across a very long room and you can control it pretty well.

Although strength isn't important in this game, small children may have trouble in getting the knack. Allow them to stand several paces closer to the hat.

Special Advice: Be sure to place the hat near a blank wall, and far away from a piano, or a sofa, or any other heavy piece of furniture. Cards that land under a piano are very hard to recover.

Treasure Hunt

Players: Any number.

Cards: 2 packs.

Preparation: Before the players arrive, hide some of the cards from one deck in one of the rooms that you devote to the game. Take out of the second deck cards that match the ones you have hidden. Make sure to hide as many red cards as black ones. A hidden card should be findable without the seeker having to move anything to get to it. For example, if you hide a card in a bookcase, it should be sticking out in some way and not hidden inside any book. Every hidden card should be well within the reach of even the youngest child. It is perfectly fair to put a card under the pedals of a piano, but not on top of the piano where a small child would be unable to see it.

The Play: When the players arrive, appoint two captains and let them choose sides. One team is to find red cards (Hearts and Diamonds), and the other team black cards (Spades and Clubs).

Give each player a card from the second deck and explain that he is to find a duplicate of it, hidden somewhere in a particular room or in two or three rooms, depending on how much space you have for the game. As soon as a player finds the card he is looking for, he is to bring it back to you and get another card to look for. The first team to find all of its hidden cards wins the game.

Be sure to explain that it isn't necessary to move anything in order to find the cards. Mention, also, that anybody who finds a card that she isn't looking for should replace that card in exactly the same spot and tell no one about it. Somebody else will be looking for it, or she herself may be looking for it later on.

This is a good game to play in somebody else's house!

2
The War Family

Most games of the War family call for the players to keep their eyes open and their brains sharp but don't require great skill in the play of the cards. Skillful players usually win, but even the youngest player has a good chance.

Slapjack

Slapjack is one of the most entertaining games that you can play with a deck of cards. It is one of the very first games that my grandfather taught me, and he didn't complain when I won from him regularly.

Players: 2 to 8. The game is best for 3 or 4 players.

Cards: 1 pack.

The Deal: One at a time to each player until all the cards have been dealt out. It doesn't matter if they don't come out even. The players square up their cards into a neat pile face down in front of them without looking at any cards.

To Win the Game: Win all the cards.

The Play: The player to the dealer's left begins by lifting the top card of her pile and dropping it *face up* in the middle of the table. The next player (to the left of the first player) does likewise—that is, he lifts the top card of *his* pile and drops it face up in the middle of the table, on top of the card that is already there. The play continues in this way, each player in turn lifting the top card of his pile and dropping it face up in the middle of the table.

As soon as any player turns up a Jack, the fun begins. The first player to slap that Jack wins the entire pile of cards in the middle of the table! If more than one player slaps at the Jack, the one whose hand is at the bottom wins the pile.

This means that you have to keep your eyes open and be pretty quick to get your hand down on a Jack. Sometimes your hand is pretty red when you're so quick that another player slaps your hand instead of the Jack, but it's all in fun. Hopefully, grownups are careful not to play too roughly!

I used to beat my grandfather all the time because he would lift his hand high in the air before bringing it down on a Jack, while I would swoop in sideways and could generally snatch the Jack away before his hand even hit the table. Grandpa never seemed to learn!

Whenever you win cards, you must put them face down underneath the cards you already have.

The play goes on until one player has won all the cards. As soon as a player has lost his last card, he may watch for the next Jack and try to slap it in order to get a new pile for himself. If he fails to get that next pile, he is out of the game. Sooner or later, all the players except one are "knocked out" in this way, and the cards all come to one player, who is the winner.

False Slaps: A player who slaps at a card that is *not* a Jack must give the top card of her pile to the owner of the card that she slapped. If the false slapper has no cards to pay the penalty, she is out.

How to Turn Cards: At your turn to play you must lift the top card of your pile and turn it *away* from you as you drop it face up in the middle of the table. This is to make sure that you don't see the card before the others do. Also, make sure that you let the card go as you drop it on the table.

Strategy: Naturally, you don't want the other players to have a big advantage, so turn the card over very quickly. Then you will see it just about as soon as they do.

Most players use the same hand for turning the cards and for slapping at Jacks. It's a more exciting game, however, if you agree that the hand used for slapping will not be the same hand used for turning the cards.

Some players use the right hand to turn over the card with a quick motion, and they swoop down on the Jack with the left hand. Other experts, since they are much swifter at swooping with the right hand, turn the card over with the left hand. You may have to try it both ways to see which is better for you.

The important thing to remember is that it's better to be a swift swooper than a slow slapper.

Snap

Players: 3 to 8—4 or 5 are best.

Cards: 1 pack.

The Deal: Any player deals one card at a time, until all the cards have been dealt. They don't have to come out even.

To Win the Game: Win all the cards.

The Play: As in *Slapjack*, each player turns up one card at a time at his turn to play. The card must be turned away from the player and dropped on the table, except that each player starts a pile in front of himself for his turned-up cards. For example, in the game for four players, after each player has had a turn, there will be four piles of face-up cards and the four packs of cards face down that were dealt at the beginning.

When a player turns up a card that matches a face-up card on any other pile, the first player to say "Snap!" wins both piles and puts them face down under her own pack.

A player who says "Snap!" at the wrong time, when the turned-up card does not match one of the other piles, must give the top card of his pile to the player who just turned up her card.

As in *Slapjack*, a player who runs out of cards may stay in for the next "Snap!" in the hope of getting a new pile. If she does not win that "Snap," she is out. A player who cries a false "Snap" is out if he has no cards to pay the penalty.

Strategy: Players have to keep looking around to make sure they know which cards are on top of the piles, since these keep changing as the game goes on. They must be ready at all times to shout "Snap!" If two or more players begin the word at the same time, the player who ends the word first, wins. This is no game for a slow talker!

My grandmother used to play this game with me. We had to make a special rule once because one little girl who was playing with us said "Snap!" every time a card was turned. She had to pay a penalty card most of the time, but this was more than offset because she won every single pile. Grandma said this wasn't fair, so we adopted the rule that after three false "Snaps" a player was out.

War

Players: 2.

Cards: 1 pack.

To Win the Game: Win all the cards.

The Play: Each player puts his stack of cards face down in front of him and turns up the top card at the same time. The player who has the higher of the two turned-up cards wins both of them and puts them face down at the bottom of his stack of cards. The King is the highest card, and the Ace is the lowest. The full rank of the cards is:

(Highest)   **(Lowest)**

Sometimes *War* is played with the Ace high.

If the two turned-up cards are of the same rank, the players have a "war." Each turns one card face down and then one card face up. The higher of the two new face-up cards takes both piles (a total of six cards).

If the newly turned-up cards again match, there is *double* war. Each player once again turns one card face down and one card face up, and the higher of these two new face-up cards wins the entire pile of ten cards.

The game continues in this way until one player has all of the cards.

This is a good game to play when you have a lot of time and nowhere to go.

War for Three

The Deal: When three players want to play *War*, take any card out of the deck and give 17 cards to each.

The Play: For the most part, the play is the same as in two-handed *War*, but when two cards turned up are the same, all three players join in the war by turning one card face down and one card face up. If two of the new turned-up cards are the same, all three players must once more turn one card down and one card face up. As usual, the highest card wins all cards that are used in the war.

   If all three turned-up cards are the same, the players must engage in double war. Each player turns two cards face down and then one card face up. If the result is a tie, all three players engage in single war.

Beat Your Neighbors Out of Doors

Other Names: Beggar My Neighbor, Strip Jack Naked

Players: 2.

Cards: 1 pack.

The Deal: Give each player half the deck.

To Win the Game: Win all the cards.

The Play: The non-dealer puts a card *face up* in the middle of the table. If it is an ordinary spot card (from the deuce up to the 10), the dealer covers it with a card from the top of his pile. This process continues, each playing one card in turn on top of the pile, until one of the players puts down an Ace, King, Queen, or Jack.

   The moment an Ace or picture card appears, the other player must pay out the proper number of cards, one at a time, face up:

> **For an Ace, four cards.**
> **For a King, three cards.**
> **For a Queen, two cards.**
> **For a Jack, one card.**

If all the cards put down for payment are spot cards, the owner of the Ace or picture card takes up the entire pile and puts it at the bottom of his stack. This is the way the cards are won, and the object of the game is to win all of them.

If, however, you turn up an Ace or picture card while you are paying out to your opponent, the payment stops and he must now pay *you* for the card that you have put down. This process continues, since either player may turn up an Ace or picture card while making a payment. Eventually, however, a player turns up only spot cards in payment, and then the entire pile is lost.

Animals

Players: 3 or more. The best game is for 5 or 6.

Cards: 1 pack.

The Deal: One card at a time until the entire deck has been dealt. It makes no difference if the cards don't come out even.

To Win the Game: Win all the cards.

The Play: Each player takes the name of an animal, such as pig, kangaroo, rhinoceros, hippopotamus.

When everybody fully understands which player represents which animal, the play begins. The player to the dealer's left turns up a card and then each player in turn turns up a card. As in *Snap*, the action takes place when a card that has just been turned up matches some other card that is face up on somebody's pile.

The players who own the matching cards must each call out the animal that the *other* represents. The first to say the other's animal name three times wins both piles.

For example, suppose three players have adopted the names Goat, Pig, and Elephant. The first turns up a Queen, the next turns up a 10, and the third turns up a Queen. The first and the third go into action, but the second must keep silent. The first shouts, "Elephant, Elephant, Elephant!" and the third shouts, "Goat, Goat, Goat!" Both piles are won by the player who finishes talking first.

Play continues until one player has all the cards.

Strategy: When some other player is about to turn up a card, make sure that you have firmly fixed in your mind the card that is at the top of your turned-up pile. And be ready to call out the other person's animal if he matches it.

When it is your own turn to turn up a card, make sure that you have looked at each of the other turned-up cards so that you can instantly spot it if you match one of them. Nine-tenths of the skill in this game lies in being alert.

As you may have noticed, it takes longer to say "Elephant, Elephant, Elephant!" than it does to say "Goat, Goat, Goat!" For this reason, it always pays to give yourself a long animal name rather than a short one. The longer it takes an opponent to say it three times, the better for you.

Good names to use are: hippopotamus, rhinoceros, elephant, mountain lion, boa constrictor, and so forth.

Farmyard

This is the same game as *Animals*, except that the players go by the noises made by a few farmyard animals instead of by the names of the animals themselves. For example, a player who chose Cow would be called "Moo-Moo-Moo" rather than "Cow, Cow, Cow." A player who chose a Duck would be called "Quack-Quack-Quack," and a player who chose Cat would be called "Meow-Meow-Meow," and so on.

I Doubt It

Other Name: Cheat

Players: 3 or more.

Cards: Use a single pack for 3 or 4 players.
Shuffle 2 packs together for 5 or more players.

The Deal: Two or three cards at a time are dealt so that each player gets an equal number of cards. When only a few cards are left, deal one at a time as far as the cards will go

To Win the Game: Get rid of all your cards.

The Play: The player to the dealer's left puts from one to four cards face down in the middle of the table, announcing that she is putting down that number of Aces. The next player puts down one to four cards and announces that he is putting down that number of deuces. The next player in turn does the same thing, stating that he is putting down that number of 3s. The play proceeds in this sequence:

(Starting)   **(Ending)**

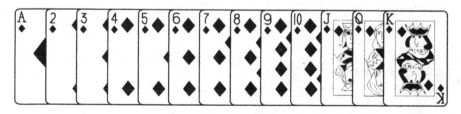

When any player puts down cards and makes his announcement, any other player may say, "I doubt it." The doubted cards must immediately be turned face up. If the statement was true, the doubter must take the entire pile into his hand. If the statement was false, the player who made the false statement must take the pile.

When the players are using two packs shuffled together, a player may put down any number of cards from one to eight.

When a player puts his last cards on the table, some other player must say, "I doubt it," since otherwise the game ends automatically. If the statement turns out to be true, the player wins the game.

25

A player who has no cards at all of the kind that she is supposed to put down is not allowed to skip her turn. She must put down one or more cards anyway and try to get away with her untruthful announcement. If somebody doubts her claim, she will have to pick up the pile.

If two or more participants say "I doubt it" at the same time, the one nearest the player's left wins the tie; that is, he picks up the pile if the statement turns out to be true after all.

Three-Card I Doubt It

The Deal: The cards are dealt out equally as far as they will go. Put any remaining cards face down in the middle of the table.

The Play: Each player in turn puts down exactly three cards. Instead of starting with Aces automatically, the first player may choose any denomination at all. For example, she may say, "Three 9s." The next player must say, "Three 10s," and so on. When a player has one or two cards left, he must draw enough cards from those put face down in the middle of the table to make up a total of three.

3
The Authors Family

In all of these games the object is to *match* cards in pairs or sets of four of a kind. A good memory will help you in some of the games, but you can have a hilarious time even if you can hardly remember your own name!

Go Fish

Players: 2 to 5.

Cards: 1 pack.

The Deal: If only two play, deal seven cards to each. If four or five play, deal five cards to each. Put the rest of the pack face down on the table, forming the stock.

To Win the Game: Form more "books" than any other player. A book is four of a kind, such as four Kings, four Queens, and so on.

The Play: The player to the dealer's left begins by saying to some other player, "(Jane), give me your *9s*." He *must* mention the name of the player he is speaking to, and he *must* mention the exact rank that he wants (Aces, Kings, Queens, and so on), and he *must* have at least one card of the rank that he is asking for.

The player who is addressed must hand over all the cards he has in the named rank, but if he has none, he says, "Go fish!"

When told to "go fish," a player must draw the top card of the stock. The turn to ask then passes to the player to his left.

If a player succeeds in getting some cards when she asks for them, she keeps her turn and may ask again. She may ask the same player or a different player, and she may ask for any rank in her new question.

If a player who has been told to "go fish" picks a card of the rank he has asked for, he shows this card immediately before putting it into his hand, and his turn continues. (In some very strict games, a player's turn would continue only if the card he fished for completed a book for him.)

Upon getting the fourth card of a book, the player shows all four, places them on the table in front of him, and continues his turn.

If a player is left without cards, she may draw from the stock at her turn and ask for cards of the same rank as the card that she has drawn. After the stock has been used up, a player who has no cards is out of the game.

The game ends when all 13 books have been assembled. The player with the most books wins.

Strategy: When a player asks for cards and gets them but does not put down a completed book, you can tell that he has either two or three of that rank. For example, suppose John requests Queens and gets one Queen from the player he has asked. John does not put down a book of Queens, but asks some new question and is told to "go fish." You now know that John held at least one Queen to give him the right to ask for Queens. He has received a Queen, which gives him a total of either two or three Queens.

In the same way, you know something about a player's hand when she asks for a card and gets nothing at all. For example, suppose Laura asks somebody for 9s and is told to "go fish" at once. You know that Laura must have at least one 9 in her hand.

Little by little, you can build up information about the cards the other players are holding. If you know that another player has Queens, but you have no Queens yourself, the information does you no good. If you have a Queen yourself, however, you are then allowed to ask for Queens, and if you ask the right person because of the information you have, you may get as many as three cards and be able to put down an entire book in front of you.

Fish for Minnows

This is a simpler way of playing *Go Fish*, and it is especially good for very young players.

The Deal: Deal out all the cards, not worrying about it if they don't happen to come out even.

To Win the Game: Accumulate the most pairs.

The Play: At his turn, a player asks for a rank, and the player who has been asked must hand over one such card, if he has one. The object is to form pairs instead of books of four. As soon as a player gets a pair, he puts them face down in front of him.

Authors

This game is a lot like *Go Fish*, but it can be played very seriously and with great skill.

Players: 2 to 5.
Cards: 1 pack.

The Deal: All 52 cards are dealt out, even though they may not come out even.

To Win the Game: Win more books than any other player. A book is four cards of the same rank.

The Play: At her turn, a player asks for a single card by naming both its rank and its suit. For example, she might say, "Bill, give me the Jack of Spades." Her turn continues if she gets the card she asked for, but it passes to the left as soon as she asks for a card that the player doesn't hold.

Old Maid

Other Name: Queen of Spades

Players: 2 or more.

Cards: 51, including only 3 of the 4 Queens.
Remove 1 Queen from the pack before beginning
the game.

The Deal: One card at a time is dealt to each player, as far as the cards will go. It doesn't matter if the cards don't come out even.

To Win the Game: Avoid getting "stuck" with the last unpaired Queen.

The Play: Each player sorts his cards and puts aside, face down, all cards that he can pair—two by two. For exanple, he might put aside two Kings, two Queens, two Jacks, and so on. If he had three Queens and three Jacks, he would be allowed to put two of them aside, but the third Jack and the third Queen would stay in his hand.

After each player has discarded his paired cards, the dealer presents her cards, fanned out but face down, to the player at her left. The player at the left selects one card (blindly, since the hand is presented face down) and quickly examines it to see if it pairs some card still in his hand. If so, he discards the pair. In any case, this player now fans his cards out and presents them face down to the player at his left.

This process continues, each player in turn presenting his hand, fanned out and face down, to the player at the left. Eventually, every card will be paired except one of the three Queens. The player who is left with the odd Queen at the end of the hand is the "Old Maid."

Whenever a player's last card is taken, he drops out. He can no longer be the "Old Maid."

Strategy: *Old Maid* can be learned in about one minute, and nothing you can do will improve your chance of winning. The player who is stuck with an odd Queen during the middle of the play usually looks worried and will often squeal with delight if the player to his left selects the Queen. If you keep alert, you can usually tell which player at the table has an odd Queen as the play is going on.

If you have the odd Queen, put it somewhere in the middle of your hand when you present it to the player at your left. Most players tend to pick a card from the middle rather than the ends. Make use of this same principle to defend yourself if you think that the player at your right has the odd Queen when he presents his hand for you to make your choice. He will usually put the Queen in the middle somewhere, and you can usually avoid choosing it by taking one of the two end cards instead.

It isn't bad to get an odd Queen toward the beginning of the play, for you will have many chances to get rid of it. It will then probably stay in some other player's hand or move only part of the way around the table.

If you like to cause a little confusion, act worried when you don't really have the Queen in your hand. Another idea is act delighted when the player to your left picks some perfectly harmless card. This will make the other players in the game believe that he has taken the odd Queen from you. You yourself will usually know where the odd Queen really is, but the other players may be in considerable doubt.

4

The Stops Family

The many games of the *Stops* family are all good fun, all easily learned, and all suitable for mixed groups of children and adults.

The simplest game of the group has no Stops at all, but it belongs in the family as a sort of great-grandfather of the other games. This game, called *Sequence*, is excellent for very young children.

Sequence

Players: 2 to 10—4 or 5 players make the best game.

Cards: 1 pack.

The Deal: One card at a time to each player until the deck is used up. It doesn't matter if some of the players are dealt more cards than the others.

To Win the Game: Get rid of all of your cards.

The Play: The player to the dealer's left puts down his lowest card in any suit he chooses. The rank of the cards is:

(Highest)   **(Lowest)**

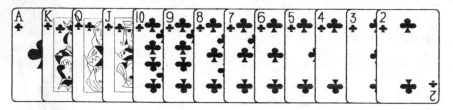

After the first card has been put down on the table, whoever has the next highest card in the same suit must put it down. This process continues until somebody finally plays the Ace of that suit.

For example, suppose that the first player's lowest Spade is the 4. He puts the 4 of Spades down on the table. Somebody else plays the 5 of Spades, and another player puts down both the 6 and the 7 of Spades (it doesn't matter if the same person plays two or more cards in a row.) This process continues until somebody finally plays the Ace of Spades.

When the Ace is reached, the one who plays it must begin a new suit. As before, the player who begins the suit must begin with her lowest card in that suit.

Sooner or later, one of the players will get rid of all of his cards. He wins the hand, and the other players lose one point for every card they still have when the hand comes to an end. (A simpler method is to forget the scoring by points and just play to win the hand.)

Strategy: Practically no skill is required for this game. It is wise, though, to begin with the deuce of some suit when it is your turn to begin a play. If you have no deuce, begin with a 3, or with the lowest card of any suit in your hand. If you don't follow this policy, you my eventually get stuck with a deuce or a 3 in your hand.

The great value of this game for very young children is that it is very easy to teach and children get practice in recognizing numbers and learning how they follow each other in sequence. For especially young children, you may want to remove the picture cards from the deck and use only the cards from 1 to 10. In this case, of course, the Ace is the lowest card, and 10 is the highest card of each suit.

Newmarket

Players: 3 to 8.

Cards: 1 pack, plus 4 special "pay cards" from another deck: the Ace of Hearts, the King of Clubs, the Queen of Diamonds and the Jack of Spades.

Equipment: A bunch of counters—poker chips, matchsticks, toothpicks, beans, etc.

Preparation: Place the pay cards in the middle of the table, where they remain throughout the game. Give each player the same number of counters. Each player puts one counter on each of the pay cards.

The Deal: The dealer gives one card at a time face down to each player, but also deals one extra hand, as though there were one more player at the table. It doesn't matter if some hands have one extra card in them.

To Win the Game: Win counters from the other players. You do this by getting rid of all your cards or by playing a pay card so you can win the counters that are placed on it.

The Auction: The dealer looks at his own hand and announces whether or not he will auction off the extra hand. If the dealer wants the extra hand himself, he puts his own hand aside, face down, and plays the extra hand in its place. If the dealer likes his own hand, he is allowed to auction off the extra hand to the player who bids the most counters for it. If two players make the same bid, the first one to speak wins. If both speak at the same time, the one who would play first going around to the left from the dealer wins the tie. Once the dealer says he is going to sell the extra hand, he is not allowed to change his mind.

The Play: The player to the left of the dealer must put down the lowest card of the suit he chooses. The player with the next higher card in the same suit continues, and the play proceeds as in *Sequence*. When any player puts down a card that is the same as one of the pay cards in the middle of the table, he collects all the counters on that card. It is therefore an advantage to hold one of these pay cards in your hand.

If a player reaches the Ace of a suit, she must start a new suit and play the lowest card she holds in that suit.

There is an important difference between this game and *Sequence*. You cannot always proceed up to the Ace of a suit, because you are sometimes stopped by the missing cards that are in the discarded hand. When no one is able to continue with a suit, the person who made the last play must begin again with a new suit, beginning (as always) with the lowest card he has in this new suit.

Sooner or later, some person plays the last card in his hand. He then collects a counter for every card left in the other players' hands.

Strategy: There is skill both in the auction and in the play. A good hand contains one or more pay cards. Even if you have no pay cards, you may still have a good chance to play out quickly if your hand contains few very low cards. It usually isn't hard to reach Queens, Kings, and Aces, but it is often very hard to get rid of deuces and 3s.

As the dealer, you may be satisfied with your hand if you have one or more pay cards, or if you have a hand that contains practically no deuces or 3s. If you have a bad hand—no pay cards and two or more very low cards—exchange your hand for the extra hand.

Follow the principle if some other player is the dealer and offers to auction off the extra hand. The extra hand isn't worth a single counter to you if you already have a good hand. If you have a bad hand, however, it is worth bidding up to three or four counters for the extra hand. If very few players are interested in bidding for the extra hand, you may get it for only one or two counters, but it probably won't be worth much. If the other players are satisfied with their hands, it is probably because they have pay cards, which means that there will be none left in the extra hand. However, there will still be an advantage in exchanging your original hand, because you will be the only player in the game who knows what cards are in the discarded hand.

In the play of the cards, it sometime helps a great deal to know when a suit is going to be stopped. For example, suppose you know that the 9 of Spades is in the dead hand. If you have the 8 of Spades in your new hand, you can safely begin Spades rather than some other suit. When you eventually play your 8 of Spades, the suit will be stopped, and you will then be able to switch to some new suit. This gives you two chances to play, so it is always an advantage to be the one who switches to a new suit.

When it is up to you to start a new suit, it is usually a sound idea to begin a suit in which you have a pay card. This is your best chance to get the pay card out of your hand and to collect the counters for playing it.

Snip, Snap, Snorem

Players: 3 or more—the more the merrier.

Cards: 1 pack.

The Deal: One at a time to each player, until the entire pack is used up. It doesn't matter if some players have more cards than the others.

To Win the Game: Get rid of all your cards.

The Play: The player to the dealer's left puts any card face up on the table. The next player to the left matches the play with the same card in a different suit, saying "Snip." The next player to the left continues to match the original play with the same card in a third suit, saying "Snap." The next player follows with the fourth card of the same kind, saying "Snorem." If a player is unable to follow with a matching card, he says "Pass," and his turn passes to the next player to the left.

For example, let's say the first player puts down a 6 of Hearts. The next player to the left has no 6 and therefore must say "Pass." The next player has the 6 of Diamonds and puts it down, saying "Snip." The next player to the left has both of the remaining 6s and therefore puts them down one at a time, saying "Snap" for the first one and "Snorem" for the second.

The player who says "Snorem," after putting down the fourth card of a kind, plays the first card of the next group of four. If he has more than one of a kind, he must put down as many as he has instead of holding out one of the cards for "Snorem." For example, if you have two Kings, you must put both of them down if you decide to play a King. You are not allowed to put down just one of the Kings and wait for the other two Kings to appear before showing your remaining King for a "Snorem."

The first player to get rid of his cards wins the game.

The Earl of Coventry

This is the same game as *Snip, Snap, Snorem* except that different words are used. The exact word depends on whether the player is young or grownup.

Young children always use the same words when putting down their cards. For example, suppose a young player puts down a five. He says, "There's as good as 5 can be." The next young player to put down a 5 can say, "There's a 5 as good as he." The next player says, "There's the best 5 of all the three." The fourth player would say triumphantly, "And there's the Earl of Coventry!"

Grownup players need to make a different rhyming statement as they play their cards. For example, an adult who plays a 5 might say, "Here's a 5 you can have from me," or "The best 5 now on land or sea," or any other rhyme.

If a grownup fails to make an acceptable rhymed statement when he plays his card, he is not allowed to begin a new play. The turn passes to the player at his left.

Jig

This is the same as *Snip, Snap, Snorem* or *The Earl of Coventry*, except that the players put down four cards in sequence instead of four of a kind.

For example, suppose that the player to the left of the dealer begins by putting down a 5. The next player must put down any 6 or must pass. The next player must put down any 7 or pass. The play is completed by the next person who puts down any 8. The one who completes the play with the fourth card in sequence then begins the new series.

The game may be played by saying "Snip, Snap, Snorem," or with rhymes, as in *The Earl of Coventry*.

Crazy Eights

Other Name: Rockaway

Players: 2 to 8. The game is best for 2, 3, or 4. In the 4-handed game, the players who sit across the table from each other are partners.

Cards: 7 to each player in a 2-handed game; 5 to each player when more than 2 are playing.

The Deal: After the correct number of cards is dealt to each player, put the rest of the cards on the table face down as the stock. Turn the top card face up to begin another pile.

To Win the Game: Get rid of all your cards. The first player to get rid of all his cards wins.

Sometimes a hand ends in a block with nobody able to play, and with nobody having played out. The hand is then won by the player with the smallest number of cards. If two or more players tie for this honor, the hand is declared a tie.

The Play: The player to the left of the dealer must match the card that has been turned up. That is, he must put down a card of the same suit or of the same rank.

For example, suppose that the card first turned up is the 9 of Spades. The first player must put down another Spade or another 9.

The newly played card is placed on top of the turned-up card. It is up to the next player to match the new card either in suit or in rank.

The four 8s are wild; that is, you may play an 8 at any time, when it is your turn. When putting down an 8, you are allowed to call it any suit at all, as you please. For example, you might put down the 8 of Hearts and say "Spade." The next player would then have to follow with a Spade.

If, at your turn, you cannot play, you must draw cards from the top of the stock until you are able to play or until there are no more cards left.. You are allowed to draw cards from the stock, at your turn, even if you are able to play *without* drawing. This is sometimes a good idea.

Strategy: The most important principle is not to play an 8 too quickly. If you waste an 8 when you are not really in trouble, you won't have it to save you when the going gets tough.

The time that you really need an 8 to protect yourself is when you have *run out of a suit*. For example, after several Spades have been played, you might not be able to get another Spade even if you drew every single card in the stock. If you are also unable to match the rank of the card that has been put down, you may be forced to pick up the entire stock before your turn is over. From here on, of course, it will be very hard for you to avoid a disastrous defeat. An 8 will save you from this kind of misfortune, since you can put it down in place of a Spade, and you may be able to call a suit that does for your opponent what the Spade would have done for you!

If you're lucky, you won't have to play an 8 at the beginning, and you can save it to play as your last card. If you're not quite as lucky as this, it is sensible to play the 8 as your next to last card. With a little luck, you will then be able to play your last card when your next turn comes—and win the hand. To play an 8 with more than two cards in your hand is seldom wise. It is usually better to draw a few cards from stock in order to find a playable card.

The best way to beat an opponent is to run her out of some suit. If you have several cards in one suit, chances are your opponent will be short in that suit. As often as you get the chance, keep coming back to your long suit until your opponent is unable to match your card. Eventually, she will have to draw from stock and may have to load herself up badly before she is able to play.

Hollywood Eights

Equipment: Paper and pencil for scoring.

This is the same as the original game of *Crazy Eights*, except that a score is kept in points with pencil and paper. When a hand comes to an end, each loser counts up his cards as follows:

Each 8	**50**
Each King, Queen, Jack, or 10	**10**
Each Ace	**1**
Each other card	**its face value**

The winner of a hand gets credit for the total of all points lost by the other players.

For example, suppose you have an 8, a 9, and a 7 when a hand ends. The 8 counts 50 points, the 9 counts 9, and the 7 counts 7. The total is 50 + 9 + 7, or 66 points.

Hollywood Scoring: Three separate game scores are kept. The first time a player wins a hand, his score is credited to him in the first game score. The second time a player wins a hand, he gets credit for his victory both in the first game and also in the second game. The third time a player wins, his score is credited to him in all three games. He continues to get credit in all three games from then on.

Sometimes the game runs on until everybody feels like stopping. In this case, the three game scores are added whenever everybody wants to stop. The winner is the player with the biggest total for the three scores.

Suppose you win five hands in a row, with scores of 10, 25, 40, 20, and 28 points. Your score would look like this:

FIRST GAME	SECOND GAME	THIRD GAME
10	5	40
(+25) 35	(+40) 65	(+20) 60
(+40) 75	(+20) 85	(+28) 88
(+20) 95	(+28) 113	
(+28) 123		

100 Scoring: A more popular method is to end a game as soon as any player's score reaches 100. When this happens in the first of the three games, the other two games continue. In the later hands, the score is entered on the second game and third games, but no further entry is made in the finished first game. Sooner or later, some player reaches a score of 100 in the second game, and this likewise comes to an end. Eventually, also, some player reaches a score of 100 in the third game, and then all three games have ended.

The winner is the player with the highest total score when all three game scores have been added up.

Go Boom

Players: 2 or more.

Cards: 1 pack.

The Deal: Seven cards are dealt to each player. The rest of the pack is put face down in the middle of the table.

To Win the Game: Get rid of all of your cards.

The Play: The player to the left of the dealer puts any card on the table. The next player to her left must follow by matching the suit or rank of that card. Each player in turn after this must match the previous card in suit or rank.

For example, suppose the first player puts down the Jack of Diamonds. The next player may follow with any Diamond or with another Jack. If the second player decides to follow with the Jack of Clubs, the third player may then match with a Club or with one of the two remaining Jacks.

When a player cannot match the previous card, he must draw cards from the stock until he is able to play. If a player uses up the stock without finding a playable card, he may say "Pass," and his turn passes to the next player.

When everybody at the table has had the chance to play or say "Pass," the cards are examined to see who has played the highest card. The cards rank as follows:

(Highest)   **(Lowest)**

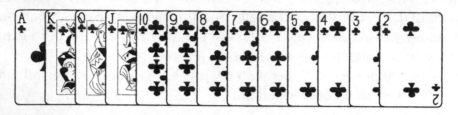

The player who put down the highest card has the right to begin the next play. If there is a tie for first place among cards of thr same rank, the card that was played first is considered higher.

The play continues in this way until one player gets rid of all of her cards. That player wins the hand.

If none of the players is very young, you might want to use a system of point scoring. When a hand comes to an end, each loser counts the cards left in his hand as follows:

Each picture card	**10**
Each Ace	**1**
Each other card	**its face value**

The winner of the hand is credited with the total of all points lost by the other players.

Strategy: The strategy in *Go Boom* is much the same as in *Crazy Eights*. You try to run your opponent out of a suit in hopes that he will not be able to match your play with a card of the same suit or the same rank.

In the early stages of play, it is useful to play as high a card as possible in order to have the best chance to win the privilege of beginning the next play.

Hollywood Go Boom

This is the same as *Go Boom*, except that the scoring is Hollywood style (three games at a time). As in *Hollywood Eights*, three game scores are kept for each player. The first time you win a hand, you get credit only in your first game score. The second time you win a hand, you get credit both in your first game score and in your second game score. After that, you get credit in all three game scores.

   The first game ends when any player reaches a score of 100. Later hands are scored only in the second and third games. The second game also ends when any player reaches a score of 100. Thereafter, the scores are entered only in the third game score, and when some player reaches a score of 100 in that game all the scores are totalled to see who wins.

Fan-Tan

Other Names: **Card Dominoes, Sevens, Parliament**

Players: **3 to 8.**

Equipment: · **A bunch of counters—poker chips, matchsticks, toothpicks, dried beans, etc.**

The Deal: One card at a time to each player until all the cards have been dealt. It doesn't matter if some players get more cards than others. Give an equal number of counters to each player.

To Win the Game: Get rid of all your cards.

The Play: To open, the player to the left of the dealer must play any 7, if possible. If not, the first player with a 7 opens. After the 7 is played, the next player to the left may play a 7 or any card in the same suit and in squence with the card previously played.

   For example, suppose that the player to the dealer's left put the 7 of Spades on the table. The next player may put down a new 7 or may play the 8 of Spades so that it covers half of the 7 of Spades. The second player, instead, might have chosen to play the 6 of Spades, putting it down also so that it just covered half of the 7 of Spades. If the 8 of Spades were played, the next player would have the right to put down the 9 of Spades. If the 9 of Spades were played, the next player would have the right to put down the 10 of Spades.

This process continues. At any turn, a player my put down a new 7 or may continue a sequence that builds up in suit from a 7 to a King or down from a 7 to an Ace. The King is the highest card that may be played on a sequence and the Ace is the lowest. If a player does not have an appropriate card, he must put a counter into the middle of the table.

The play continues until one player gets rid of all of his cards. That player then collects all the counters in the middle of the table. In addition, each loser pays out one counter for every card left in her hand.

Strategy: It is usually easy to get rid of cards of middle size, such as 8s, 9s, 6s or 5s. It is usually hard to get rid of very low or very high cards, such as Aces and deuces or Queens and Kings.

The best tactic is to force the other players to build up to your high cards or down to your low cards. You can't always carry it off, but you can try.

If you have the 8 of Spades, nobody can play the 9 of Spades or any higher Spade until you have first put down your 8. If a player who has high Spades finds no chance to play them, he must play something else at his turn. This other play may be just what you need to reach your own very low cards or your own very high cards.

This shows you the general strategy. Play as much as possible in the suit that will lead to your very high cards or to your very low ones. Wait as long as possible before playing in the suits in which you have only middle-rank cards. With just a little luck, you will get rid of your very high cards and your very low cards fairly early. You will then be able to get rid of your middle-rank cards in the last suit, catching the other players while they still have the very high and very low cards in that suit.

Liberty Fan-Tan

This is the same game as *Fan-Tan*, except that it isn't necessary to begin a suit by playing the 7. Nobody can start a new suit until the previous suit has been finished.

The player to the left of the dealer begins by playing any card of any suit. The next player must follow with the next higher card in the same suit or must put one counter in the middle of the table. The third player must continue with the next card in sequence or must put one counter in the middle of the table. This process continues, building up past the King with the Ace, deuce, and so on, until all 13 cards of the suit have been played. The one who plays the 13th card of the first suit may begin with any card in a new suit. Then the same process continues with a second suit.

The first player to get rid of all of her cards takes all the counters from the pool.

Strategy: Your chance of winning is best when you can determine which suit will be played last. If you have very few cards in this suit, you have an excellent chance to win all the counters since you will get rid of your cards while the other players still have cards of that suit left.

The time to choose the last suit does not come after the third suit has been played, since at that point there is no choice. The choice is made after the second suit has been played, since then two suits remain. The player who chooses the third suit automatically fixes the other suit as the fourth.

If you happen to end the second suit, by good luck, you will then begin the play of the third. Naturally, you should play your longer suit, saving your shorter suit for last.

If the two suits are almost equal in length, it is sometimes wiser to play the shorter suit third and save the other suit for the last. The time to do this is when you have two cards in sequence in the shorter suit. If you start with the higher of these two cards, you will naturally be the one to finish the suit when yoy play the lower card.

For example, suppose you have a hand with Spades:

You notice that the 9 and 8 are in sequence. Following the principle just mentioned, you would begin the suit by playing the 9. Other players would follow with the 10, Jack and Queen, allowing you to play the King. Then someone would play the Ace and you would follow with the 2. The others would then play on until your eight would complete the suit. Having completed the suit, it is up to you to start the next suit, and this is exactly what you had in mind.

Use the same strategy of starting the second suit with the higher card if you have two cards in sequence. This will allow you to end the second suit and choose the third

Five or Nine

This is the same as *Fan-Tan*, except that the first player may put down a 5 or a 9 (instead of a 7). The card chosen by the first player sets the pattern for the rest of that hand. If he puts down a 5, for example, the other three suits must also begin with 5s; and if the first player begins by putting down a 9, the other three suits must be started by 9s.

Regardless of how the play begins, each suit builds up to a King as its top card and down to an Ace.

Commit

Players: 4 or more.

Cards: 1 pack.

Equipment: A bunch of counters—poker chips, matchsticks, toothpicks, dried beans, etc.

The Deal: Remove the 8 of Diamonds from the pack. Deal the cards one at a time as far as thay will go evenly. Put the remaining cards face down in the middle of the table. Give an equal number of counters to each player.

To Win the Game: Get rid of all your cards.

The Play: The player to the dealer's left may put any card down on the table. She and the other players can then build up in sequence in the same suit.

For example, suppose that Gina begins with the 7 of Clubs. Any player who has the 8 of Clubs puts it face up on the table. Then it is the turn of any player who has the 9 of Clubs. This continues until someone plays the King of Clubs or until the sequence is stopped because the next card is one of those face down in the middle of the table —or the 8 of Diamonds, which has been removed.

When the play stops for either of these reasons, the person who played last begins a new sequence with any card in his hand.

The 9 of Diamonds is a special card in this game. You can of course play it when you end a sequence and it is your turn to begin a new one. But you can also play it in the middle of any sequence. When the 9 of Diamonds is played, each player in turn has the chance to proceed either with the 10 of Diamonds—continuing the Diamond sequence— or with the sequence that was interrupted by the 9 of Diamonds.

For example, suppose that Avery begins a sequence with the 3 of Spades. Barbara puts down the 4 of Spades and then follows it with a 9 of Diamonds. Chris, the player to the left, then has a choice to make. She may continue with a 10 of Diamonds, or go back to the 5 of Spades. If she has neither card, the turn passes on to the left until somebody plays either the 10 of Diamonds or the 5 of Spades, which determines how the sequence will continue.

When you play the 9 of Diamonds, you collect two counters from every player in the game. If anyone gets rid of all of his cards before you have played the 9 of Diamonds, you must *pay* two counters to every player in the game.

When a player wins the game (by playing all his cards), the remaining players must show their hands. Any player who has a King must pay one counter to every other player in the game.

Strategy: As in the game of *Newmarket*, the best strategy is to begin with your lowest card in your longest suit.

It is helpful to remember the stops. At the beginning of a hand, the only stop you are sure of is the 8 of Diamonds. It pays to begin with a low Diamond if you have the 7 of Diamonds in your hand, for then you will probably build up to that 7 and have the chance to begin the next sequence.

Rolling Stone

Players: 4 to 6.

Cards: When 4 play, use the Ace, King, Queen, Jack, 10, 9, 8, and 7 of each suit. If there is a fifth player, add the 6s and 5s. If there is a sixth player, add the 4s and 3s. There must be 8 cards for each player.

The Deal: One card at a time until each player has eight cards. This uses up the pack.

To Win the Game: Get rid of all your cards.

The Play: The player to the dealer's left begins by putting down any card he pleases. Then the play moves to the left and the next player puts down another card in the same suit. The turns continue, always moving to the left, with the other players following with another card of the same suit, if they can, playing high or low, as they please.

If all the cards in a suit are played, the person who put down the highest card leads again. And all the cards that were played to the first "trick" (sequence of cards) are turned over and put aside.

When a player cannot put down a card of the same suit when it is her turn to play, she must pick up all the cards previously played in that sequence. This ends the trick, and the player who picks up the cards then begins the next trick by leading with any card she chooses.

The process continues. In most games a player picks up the cards several times. Eventually, one player will get rid of all his cards, and win the hand.

For the purpose of winning a trick, the cards rank as follows:

(Highest)   **(Lowest)**

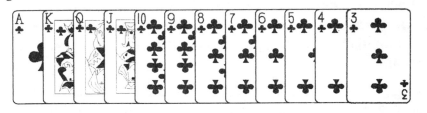

Play or Pay

Players: 3 or more.

Equipment: A handful of counters—poker chips, matchsticks, toothpicks, dried beans, etc.

The Deal: One card at a time to each player, until the pack has been used up. It doesn't matter if some players get more cards than others. Give an equal number of counters to each player.

To Win the Game: Get rid of all your cards.

The Play: The player to the left of the dealer may put down any card from her hand. The player to her left must follow with the next highest card in the same suit—or must put a counter into the middle of the table. This process continues, with each player in turn either putting down the next card or paying one counter.

The cards in their proper sequence are:

and so on.

The player who puts down the 13th card of a suit makes the first play in the next suit.

Keep on playing until someone wins by getting rid of all his cards. Each player then puts one counter in the middle of the table for each card left in his hand. The winner takes all the counters from the middle of the table.

Strategy: There is no skill in following suit; you either have the card or you don't. The only skill is in choosing the right card with which to begin a play.

If you have two cards in sequence in any suit, begin with the one that is higher in rank. Eventually, you will end that suit by playing the lower card of the sequence. This will give you the right to begin the next suit.

When possible, try to get rid of your long suits first.

5
The Casino Family

Games of the Casino family have been favorites of adults and children for hundreds of years. They are especially recommended by educators because they teach painlessly the first lessons in arithmetic.

Casino

Players: 2 to 4—best for 2.

Cards: 1 pack.

The Deal: The deck of 52 cards is used up in six deals. In the first deal:

>The non-dealer receives two cards face down.
>Then two cards are put face up on the table.
>Then the dealer gives himself two cards face down.

And the process repeats, so that each player and the table have four cards each. In the remaining five deals, the dealer continues to give each player four cards—two at at time—but does not give any additional cards to the table.

To Win the Game: Get the highest number of points. You get points by capturing the most cards, the most Spades, Aces, the 10 of Diamonds (Big Casino) and the 2 of Spades (Little Casino). See "Scoring."

The Play: Beginning with the non-dealer, each player in turn must play one card from her hand, until all four of her cards are gone. If she can find no better use for it, she simply lays her card face up on the table. This is called *trailing*. Whenever she can, though, she uses her card to capture cards from the table.

Pairing: You may win cards in various ways. The simplest is by pairing. You may capture a card on the table by another of the same rank from your hand—a 5 with a 5, a Jack with a Jack, and so on.

With a picture card—a Jack, Queen or King—you may capture only one card, but with a card of lower rank, you may take two or three of the same kind at the same time. If there are two 7s on the table and you have a 7 in your hand, for example, you can take all three 7s.

Each player keeps captured cards in a pile, face down.

Building: All the lower cards, Ace to 10, may be captured by building. Ace counts as 1. Each other card counts as its own value. Cards on the table may be taken in by higher cards to equal their sum.

For example, you may take a 5 and a 2 with a 7—or an Ace and a 9 with a 10. You may, at the same time, take additional cards by pairing. Suppose that the cards on the table are 9, 8, 5, 4, Ace. You could take them all with a single 9, since the 9s pair, 8 and 1 make 9, and 5 and 4 make 9.

Leaving a Build: Suppose that you have 8 and 3 in your hand and there is a 5 on the table, You may put the 3 on the 5 and say, "Building 8." Your intention is to capture the build with your 8 on your next turn. You cannot build and capture in the same turn, because you are allowed to play only one card from your hand at a time.

If your opponent has an 8, she can capture your build. That is the risk of leaving a build. Yet the risk is usually worth taking, because in building, you make it harder for your opponent to capture the cards. She cannot take the 5 or the 3 by pairing or by making a build of her own.

Of course, you may not leave a build unless you have a card in your hand that can take it. You *are*, however, allowed to duplicate your build before taking it in. Suppose you have two 8s in your hand. After building the 5 and 3, you could on your next turn simply put one 8 on the build, and take it with the other 8 on your third turn.

Or suppose after you build the 5 and 3, your opponent trails a 6, and you have a 2 in your hand (besides the 8). You may take your 2 and put it—with the 6— on the 5-3 build and wait until your next turn to take in the duplicated build.

An important rule is that when you have left a build on the table, you must deal with it at your next turn—take it in—or increase or duplicate it. You are not allowed to trail or to take in other cards instead.

Increasing a Build: Suppose that your opponent has laid a 4 from her hand on a 5 on the table and called out, "Building 9." You have an Ace and a 10. You may add the Ace to her build and say, "Building 10." You are allowed to increase a build of your own, in the same way.

But there are two restrictions on increasing a build. First, you may increase only a *single* build, such as the 5-4, not one that has been duplicated in any way, such as 5-4-9. Second, the card you use to increase it must come from your hand; you are not allowed to use a card from the table.

Scoring: After the last card of the sixth deal is played, any cards remaining on the table go to the player who was last to capture cards. Then each player looks through his captured cards and counts his score, as follows:

Cards, for winning 27 or more cards	3	points
Spades, for winning seven or more Spades	1	
Big Casino, the 10 of Diamonds	2	
Little Casino, the 2 of Spades	1	
Aces, each counting 1, total	<u>4</u>	
	11	

The first one to reach a total of 21 or more points wins.

Spade Casino

This is *Casino* with a different count for Spades. Instead of getting one point for having seven or more Spades, the Spades score as follows;

Jack	2
Little Casino	2
Other Spades	1 each

There are 24 points to be won. The game is usually set at 61 and scored on a Cribbage board.

Sweep Casino

This is *Casino* with the additional rule that a player scores one point for each *sweep*. You can earn this by capturing all the cards that are on the table at any one time. To keep track of sweeps, turn the top card of each sweep face up.

Winning the cards left on the table after the last deal does not count as a sweep.

Pirate Casino

The "pirate" feature is that you are allowed to make any play you please at a time when you have left a build on the table. You may take in other cards, or even trail.

Stealing Bundles

This is *Casino* for the very young. Cards may be captured only by pairing, but any number of the same kind may be taken at a time. Captured cards must be kept in a pile face up, and you can capture your opponent's entire pile by matching its top card with a card from your hand.

To Win the Game: Win more than half the cards.

Royal Casino

Children often prefer this colorful elaboration on the basic game. Since *Royal Casino* is more complicated, young children should learn the basic game before attempting it.

In this game you may capture face cards as well as lower cards two, three, and four at a turn. Furthermore, they can be used to capture builds:

Jack counts	11
Queen counts	12
King counts	13
Ace counts	14 or 1, as you please
Big Casino	10 or 16
Little Casino	2 or 15

Sweeps are scored, as in *Sweep Casino*.

Partnership Casino

Players: 4, the two opposite being partners.

Cards: 1 pack.

The Deal: The deck is used up in three deals. In the first, each player receives four cards and four are dealt face up on the table. For the other two deals, each receives four more cards, but no more are dealt to the table.

Otherwise, this game is played just like *Casino* (basic or *Royal*), except that you may duplicate a build left by your partner without you yourself having a card that can take it.

For example, if Tom builds 10, Nellie, his partner, may in turn put a 6 from the table and a 4 from her hand on the build, without having a 10 in her hand.

Draw Casino

You can play either basic *Casino* or *Royal Casino* in "Draw" style. After you deal, place the rest of the pack face down in the middle of the table. Each time you play a card, draw the top card of this stock, so that you keep four cards in your hand throughout the game. After the stock is exhausted, play out the hands as usual.

6
The Rummy Family

Rummy is the most widely played of all card games. Many different forms of the game are played, but all have a very strong family resemblance, Once you have learned to play the basic game, you can pick up any variation in a few minutes.

Basic Rummy

Players: 2 to 6.

Cards: 10 each when 2 play.
7 each when 3 or 4 play.
6 each when 5 or 6 play.

Equipment: Pencil and paper for keeping score.

The Deal: Deal the appropriate number of cards to each player and then put the rest of the cards face down in the middle of the table, forming the stock. Turn the top card face up, starting the discard pile.

In a two-handed game, the winner of each hand deals the next hand. When more than two play, the turn to deal passes to the left exactly as the cards are dealt out.

To Win the Game: Win points from your opponents. You usually keep track of these points with a pencil and paper score.

In order to win points, you must match up your cards. One way to match is to get three or four of a kind. For example, you might have three Kings or four 10s and so on.

A second way to match is to get sequences—cards that are next to each other in rank and are in the same suit. The rank of the cards in *Rummy* is:

(Highest)   **(Lowest)**

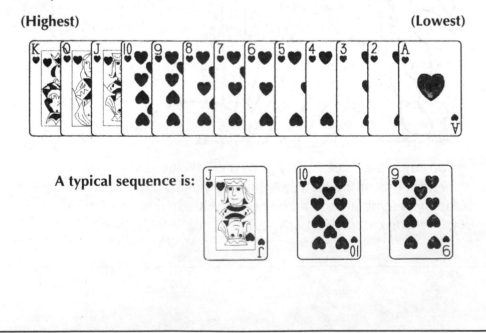

A typical sequence is:

60

Another typical sequence is: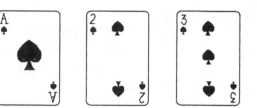

You need at least three cards for a sequence.

The Play: Each player at the table plays in turn, beginning with the player to the dealer's left. During your turn to play, you do three things

> **You draw.**
> **You meld (if you wish to do so).**
> **You discard.**

When you draw, you may pick up the top card of the stock or the top card of the discard pile. You add this card to your hand.

You meld by putting a group of matched cards down on the table. For example, you might put down three of a kind or four of a kind, or a sequence. You might even put down two groups of matched cards, if you are lucky enough to have them in your hand. You are not required to expose your meld if you don't wish to do so. You can keep it in your hand.

After some other player has melded, you may add to his meld when it's your turn. For example, if some player has put down three Kings, you may add the fourth King at your turn to play. If some player has put down the 6, 7 and 8 of Diamonds, you may add the 9 and 10 of Diamonds, or just the 9 or the 5 or 5 and 4, or any such card or group of cards. You may add to a meld that has been put down previously by any player at the table—including yourself.

After you have drawn and melded (or after you have declined to meld), it is your turn to discard. You take any card from your hand and put it on top of the face-up pile in the middle of the table. This completes your play.

When, at your turn to play, you manage to meld all your cards, you win the game. You must begin your play with a draw, thus adding one card to your hand, and then you must meld either all the cards in your hand or all but one. If you meld all but one card, that last card is your discard.

If no player has melded all his cards (called *going out*) by the time the stock is used up, the next player may take either the top card of the discard pile or the top card of the new stock that has been formed by turning the discard pile over. In either case, play continues as before until somebody does go out.

Scoring: The winner of a hand scores points by counting up the hands of all the other players in the game. Each loser counts his cards according to the following scale:

Picture cards	**10 points each**
Aces	**1 point each**
Other cards	**their face value**

A loser does not count cards that he has previously melded on the table, but he does count any cards that remain in his hand—*whether or not these cards match!*

A player goes "Rummy" when he melds all his cards in one turn, without previously melding or adding to anybody else's meld. A player may go "Rummy" by melding all his cards after the draw, or he may meld all but one and then discard that last card. Whenever a player goes "Rummy," he wins double the normal amount from each of the other players.

A score is kept on paper with a column for each player in the game. Whenever a player wins a hand, the amounts that he wins from the other players are put into his winning column.

Some players agree on a stopping time when they play *Rummy.* The winner of a game is the player who has the highest score when the agreed-upon time comes.

Other players end a game when any player reaches a certain total score, such as 500 points.

The score for each player is added up at the end of each hand.

Strategy: In all games of the *Rummy* family, you try to build up your hand by keeping cards that match and by discarding cards that do not match.

For example, if you drew the 10 of Spades, you would tend to keep it if your hand contained one or more 10s, or the Jack of Spades or the 9 of Spades. In such cases, your 10 of Spades might be a useful card. Even if it did not immediately give you a meld, it would probably bring you closer to one.

If you drew a card that did not match anything in your hand, you would either discard it immediately or wait for a later chance to do so.

If the player to your left picks a card from the discard pile, this gives you a clue to his hand. If, for example, he picks up the 9 of Diamonds, you know that he must have other 9s or other Diamonds in the neighborhood of the 9. If convenient, you would avoid throwing another 9 or another Diamond in that vicinity onto the discard pile. This is called *playing defensively*. You don't need to bother with defensive play against anybody but the player to your left, since your discard would be covered up by the time any *other* player wanted to draw.

The advantage of melding is that you cannot lose the value of those cards even if some other player wins the hand.

The advantage of holding a meld in your hand is that nobody can add to the meld while it is still in your hand. A second advantage is the possibility of going "Rummy" all in one play.

It sometimes pays to hold up a meld, but most successful *Rummy* players make it a habit to put melds down fairly quickly. It is usually safe to hold ip a meld for one or two turns, but after that it becomes dangerous. If another player goes out before you have melded, you will lose those matched cards just as though they were unmatched.

Block Rummy

This is the same as *Basic Rummy*, except that the discard pile is not turned over to begin as stock again. When the stock has been used up, the next player has the right to take the top card of the discard pile. If she does not wish to take it, the hand ends immediately. This is called a *block*.

When a block occurs, each player shows his hand. The player with the lowest number of points in his hand wins the difference in count from each of the other players. If two or more players tie for the low number of points, they share the winning equally.

Boathouse Rummy

This is like *Basic Rummy*, except that sequences go "around the corner." For example, you may meld:

as a sequence. But you are not allowed to meld anything at all until you can meld your whole hand and go out. When you go out, you win points from every other player according to his *unmatched* cards—that is, the cards in his hand that he has not matched up in groups of three or four or in squences.

Scoring: There are two methods. One is to count one point for each unmatched card.

The other is to count

11	**for an unmatched Ace**
10	**for a face card**
face value	**for all other cards**

One other peculiarity of *Boathouse Rummy* is in the draw. When you begin your turn, if you draw the top card of the discard pile, you may then draw a second card—from the discard pile or the stock, whichever you please. If you begin by drawing from stock, however, you don't get a second card.

Contract Rummy

Other Name: Liverpool Rummy

Players: 3 to 8.

Cards: 2 packs of 52 cards plus 1 Joker, for 3 or 4 players.
3 packs plus 2 Jokers, for 5 or more players.

Equipment: Paper and pencil for keeping score.

The Deal: Deal 10 cards to each player, except in Deal 7, when each player receives 12. Put the rest of the cards face down in the middle of the table, forming the stock. Turn the top card of the stock face up beside it, starting the discard pile.

To Win the Game: Get rid of all the cards in your hand by melding them.

Melds: The melds are as in *Basic Rummy:*
groups of three or four cards of the same rank, such as Queens;
sequences of three or more cards of the same suit, such as:

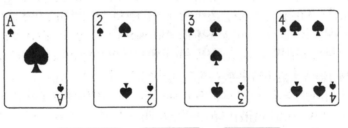

The Contract: A game consists of seven deals. In each deal, a player's first meld must be a combination of two or three sets according to this schedule:

Deal 1:	**two groups**
Deal 2:	**one group and one sequence**
Deal 3:	**two sequences**
Deal 4:	**three groups**
Deal 5:	**two groups and a sequence**
Deal 6:	**one group and two sequences**
Deal 7:	**three sequences**

When you meld in Deals 1—6, you may put down only three cards per set. If you have additional matching cards, you may put them down at any later turn.

In Deal 7, however, you must meld all 12 cards at once, thus going out.

The Play: As in *Basic Rummy*, a turn consists of a draw, melding (if you wish), and a discard.

If you, the first player, decide not to draw the top card of the discard pile, you must say so. Then any other player who wants it may take it. If two or more want it, the person nearest you (to the left) is entitled to it. He must pay for the privilege of taking the discard out of turn, though, by drawing the top card of the stock also. He must then await his regular turn before melding or discarding. Then you resume your turn, drawing the top card of the stock.

Your first meld of any kind must be the *contract.* After that, you are not allowed to meld any new sets, but you may add matching cards to any sets on the table—yours and the other players'.

A peculiarity of the game is that a sequence may be built to the Ace both ways, making a set of 14 cards. (Of course, this rarely happens.)

Wild Cards: The Joker is wild. You may call it any card you please, to help you get rid of cards by melding. You must say, though, what card it represents.

For example, if you put the Joker down with the 7 of Spades and the 7 of Diamonds, you must say either "7 of Hearts" or "7 of Clubs." The reason for this is shown by the next rule. A player who holds the named card may, in her turn, put it down in place of the Joker, thus getting the Joker for her own use.

Many players like to have additional wild cards, to make it easier to form sets for the contract. Deuces are often used as wild, but a deuce cannot be captured, as a Joker can. However, if a deuce is melded in a sequence, any player may put the natural card in its place and move the deuce to either end of the sequence.

Ending Play: Play continues until somebody goes out. If the stock is exhausted, the discard pile is turned over without shuffling.

Scoring: The player who goes out scores zero—which is good! Each other player scores the total of the cards left in his hand. Aces and wild cards count 15 each, picture cards are 10, other cards count their face value. The player with the *lowest* total score after Deal 7 wins the game.

Knock Rummy

Players: 2 to 6.

Cards: 10 cards to each player when 2 play.
7 cards to each player when 3 or 4 play.
5 cards to each player when 5 or 6 play.

Equipment: Paper and pencil for keping score.

The Play: The play follows *Basic Rummy*, but there is no melding until somebody knocks. To "knock" means to lay down your whole hand face up, ending the play. You may knock in your turn, after drawing but before discarding. You do not have to have a single meld to knock—but you had better be convinced that you have the *low* hand.

When anybody knocks, all players lay down their hands, arranged in such melds as they have, with the *unmatched* cards separate. What counts is *the total of unmatched cards*.

If the knocker has the lowest count, he wins the difference of counts from each other player.

If he lays down a *rum hand*—one with no unmatched card—he wins an extra 25 points from everybody, besides the count of unmatched cards held by the others.

If somebody beats or ties the knocker for low count, that player wins the difference from everybody else.

When the knocker is beaten, he pays an extra penalty of 10 points.

It's best to keep score with paper and pencil. Each item should be entered twice—*plus* for the winner and *minus* for the loser.

Tunk

Players: 2 to 5.

Cards: 1 pack with 2 or 3 players.
2 packs with 4 or 5 players.

The Deal: Each player receives seven cards.

The Play: The rules follow *Basic Rummy*, and the object is to go out.

Deuces are wild and may be used in place of natural cards to form melds.

To go out, you don't need to meld all your cards, but merely reduce the total of your unmatched cards to five or less. Before going out, you must give notice by saying "Tunk," in your turn—and that is all you can do in that turn. A tunk takes the place of draw-meld-discard. Then the other players unload all that they can from their hands, and on your next turn you lay down your hand, ending the play. You may at any time add cards to your own melds, or to a tunker's melds after the tunk, but not on another player's.

The tunker scores zero, and the others are charged with the count of all cards left in their hands. When a player reaches 100, he is out of the game, and the others play on until there is only one survivor.

Gin Rummy

Gin is one of the best and also one of the most popular of the *Rummy* games.

Players: 2.

Cards: **A regular pack of 52. The ranking is:**

(Highest)   **(Lowest)**

Equipment: **Pencil and paper for keeping score.**

The Deal: Each player receives 10 cards, dealt one at a time. Place the rest of the deck face down in the middle of the table to form the stock. Turn over the top card of the stock beside it. This *upcard* starts the discard pile.

The Play: The non-dealer plays first. If she wants the upcard, she may take it, but if she doesn't want it, she must say so without drawing. Then the dealer may take the upcard, if he wishes, and discard one card from his hand, face up. After he has taken or refused it, the non-dealer continues with her turn, drawing one card—the top card of the stock or the new top of the discard pile. Then she must discard one card face up on the discard pile. The turns alternate and there are no further complications.

To Win the Game: Reduce the count of your unmatched cards.

A "matched set" in *Gin* is the same as a "meld" in *Basic Rummy*—three or four cards of the same rank, or three or more cards in sequence in the same suit.

For example, here are two matched sets:

Since, in *Gin*, Aces rank low:

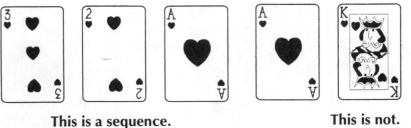

This is a sequence.   **This is not.**

The point values are:

Ace:	1
Picture cards:	10
Other cards:	face value

Knocking: All melding is kept in the hand until some player brings matters to a halt by laying down all his 10 cards either by "ginning" or by "knocking."

To gin, you lay down all your cards in melds. When you knock, you have unmatched cards whose total is 10 or less. You may knock only when it is your turn to play, after drawing and before discarding. The final discard is made *face down*, thereby indicating the intention to knock. If you simply place the card face up, intending to lay down your hand, you could be stopped, because—according to the rules—the face-up discard ended your turn.

As you play, you arrange your cards in matched sets with the un-matched cards to one side. It is customary to announce the total count of your unmatched cards by saying something like, "Knocking with five," or "I go down for five." Your opponent then exposes her hand, arranged by matched sets and unmatched cards. She is entitled to lay off cards on your sets, provided that you don't have a *gin hand*—all 10 cards matched.

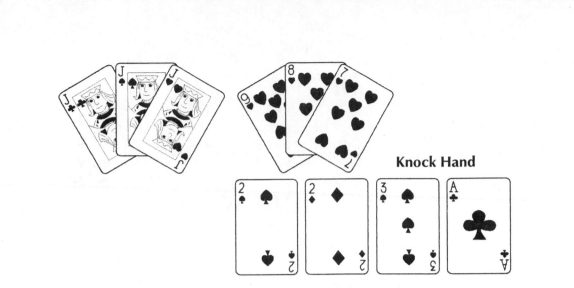

Knock Hand

For example, if you had the hand shown, your opponent could lay off the fourth Jack, and the 10 and 6 of Hearts, if she had any of these cards.

Scoring: Your opponent counts her remaining unmatched cards, after laying off what she can on your hand. If this count is higher than yours, you win the difference. If your opponent has the same count that you have—or a lower one—she scores the difference (if any), plus 25 points for *undercutting* you.

If you lay down a gin hand, your opponent may not lay off any cards on it. You win the opponent's count, plus a bonus of 25 points. This bonus cannot be won when you knock. Suppose, for example, you play 'possum with a gin hand until your opponent knocks with one point or more. You would win her count, plus 25 for undercutting, but you don't get the bonus for a gin hand.

Keepng Score: Keep score with pencil and paper. Enter the net result of a hand in the column under the winner's name, draw a line below the item, and then write the running total. The lines between items are important, to keep track of how many hands were won by each player.

The first player to reach a total of 100 or more wins the game. You score a bonus of 100 for winning and an additional 100 for a *shutout*—also called "whitewash," "skunk," "Schneider," "goose-egg," etc.—if your opponent has not scored a single point. Then each player is credited with 25 pints for each winning hand. This is called the *line* or *box* score. The winner then carries forward the difference between his own grand total and his opponent's.

Hollywood Gin

This is *Gin* with Hollywood scoring (see pages 42-43).

Oklahoma Gin Rummy

This is simply *Gin*, except that the upcard determines the maximum number with which you may knock.

For example, if you turn up a 3 from the stock, it takes 3 or less to knock in that deal.

If you turn up a 10 or a picture card, the game is no different from regular *Gin*. Some players like to pep up the game with additional rules, such as: The hand counts double when the upcard is a Spade.

Around-the-Corner Gin

This is *Gin* again, except that sequences may go "around the corner."

For example, this sequence is a matched set.

An unmatched Ace counts as 15 points. The person who doesn't knock may lay off cards even on a gin hand. The game is usually set at 125 points.

500 Rummy

The chief feature of *500 Rummy* is that you score for melding as well as for going out.

Other Name: Sequence Rummy

Players: 3 to 8.

Cards: When more than 4 play, use 2 packs of 52 shuffled together.

Equipment: Paper and pencil for keeping score.

The Deal: Seven cards go to each player. The deal passes to the left.

The Play: As in *Basic Rummy*, you may begin your turn by drawing the top card of the stock or the discard pile. But you have a third choice of drawing *any* card in the discard pile, no matter how deeply it is buried. You must immediately meld this card. You must also pick up all the cards that cover it and add them to your hand. You then proceed to meld all the cards you wish to. Your turn ends when you discard.

Discards are not stacked in a pile as in most Rummy games, but are spread out in an overlapping fan so that all the cards can be seen. It is of course important not to mix up the order in which they lie. When you "dig deep" into the discards, courtesy requires that you leave cards on the table for awhile to give the other players a chance to see what you're getting.

Melds are made as in *Basic Rummy*. You may add cards to your own melds and also to those belonging to other players.

Play ends when some player gets rid of all his cards, with or without making a final discard. If nobody goes out by the time the stock is exhausted, play continues as long as each player in turn draws from the discard pile, but it ends as soon as any player fails to do so.

Scoring: When play ends, each player counts up the difference between the cards he has melded and the cards left in his hand. This difference (which may be plus or minus) is added to his running total score, which is kept on paper.

The cards count as follows:

Ace	**15 or 1, if it was melded in a low sequence**
Picture cards	**10 each**
Other cards	**face value**

The first player to score 500 points wins the game.

Strategy: Much more is won by melding than by going out. Try to meld as much as possible, and to meld high cards rather than low ones. For this purpose, you'll want to get as many cards into your hand as you can. The deeper you have to dig into the discard pile, the happier you'll be!

If you are dealt a low meld, such as three deuces, discard one of them as soon as you can. Then, after the discard pile has grown to 10 or 12 cards, reclaim your deuce to meld it—and get some booty! Just don't be too greedy; if you wait too long, somebody else may take the pile, for you can be sure that the others will "salt" the pile too, if they have the chance.

At the beginning of a game, try to avoid making it too easy for another player to take the discard pile. You may make it easy if you discard a card that pairs with another already in the pile, or that is in suit and sequence with one in the pile. Of course, there comes a time when you have no more safe discards. Then follow the principal of doing the least damage. Discard a card that may let another player take a *few* cards, rather than a great many.

As a rule, don't meld unless you have to in order to dig into the discard pile. Keeping a meld of high cards in your hand, especially Aces, puts the fellow who has the fourth Ace on the spot. If he discards it, he gives you a chance to pick up the pile; if he holds it, he may get stuck with it. If you meld your Aces, his troubles are over. If you are too lavish in melding, you may help another player go out.

You need to be quick to switch your tactics, however, when the stock is nearly gone or when another player reduces his hand to only a few cards. That's the time to meld your high cards, to be sure that they will count *for* you instead of against you.

7
Trump Games

A trump suit is one that is given a special privilege: it can take all the other suits. For example, if Spades are trumps, a Spade will win over any Heart, Club, or Diamond. The deuce of Spades then can take the Ace of Hearts, although the Ace of Hearts can win over any lower Heart.

In some games, the trump suit is determined by turning up a card from the deck—its suit becomes trump. In other games, the right to name the trump suit is decided by the players *bidding*. It goes to the player who is willing to pay most for that right. Players *bid* what they are willing to pay—a number of counters to be put in a pool, for example. Usually, each bidder names a number of points or tricks that she hopes to win. The one who names the trump must win at least what she has bid, in order to advance her score. If she fails, points are taken away from her or her opponent's score (according to the particular game). Failing to make a bid goes by different names in different games—"set," "euchre," "bate," and so on.

Linger Longer

A good way to start learning trump games.

Players: 4 to 6.

Cards: **Each player receives as many cards as there are players in the game. For example, with 5 players, each receives 5 cards.**

The Deal: The last card dealt, which goes to the dealer, is shown to all the players. It decides the trump suit for that trick. The rest of the deck is placed face down in the middle of the table, forming the stock.

The Play: The player to the left of the dealer makes the first *lead* (play), putting down in the middle of the table any card in the trump suit, if he can. Otherwise, he may put down whatever card he pleases. The other players must *follow suit*, putting down any cards in their hand that match the suit of the first lead.

The cards are played in "tricks." Each player tries to capture the trick of four cards by playing the highest trump, or, if there is no trump, by the highest card played of the suit that was led.

When a player wins a trick, he "owns" those cards and draws the top card of the stock. That card determines the trump suit for the next trick. When a player is left without any cards, he has to drop out of the game, and the others play on.

To Win the Game: To get all the cards and be the last player left when everyone else has dropped out. If two or more players are down to one card each at the end, the winner of the last trick wins the game.

Napoleon

Other Name: Nap

Players: 2 to 6.

Cards: A regular pack of 52.

Equipment: A handful of counters—poker chips, matchsticks, toothpicks, dried beans, etc.

The Deal: Each player receives five cards, one at a time. Give out the counters, the same number to each player.

The Bidding: The player to the left of the dealer has the first turn. He "bids" (predicts) the number of tricks he will take if he is allowed to name the trump suit. Each player has one turn in which he may pass or may bid from one to five. A bid of five tricks is called "nap."

The Play: The highest bidder names the trump suit and makes the first lead, which must be a trump.

The cards are played in tricks. The players must *follow suit* to the lead card if they can. Otherwise, there is no restriction on what they may play or lead.

The winner of each trick leads to the next trick—playing any suit—and everyone continues to follow that lead. The trick is won by the highest card. The bidder tries to win the number of tricks she has named. All the other players combine forces against her. Play stops the moment the outcome is sure—success or defeat for the bidder.

Scoring: When a bidder wins, she collects from each other player the same number of counters as her bid. If she is defeated, she pays this number to each player.

The bid of nap" for all the tricks is special. If you make it, you collect 10 counters from each player, but if you fail, you pay five to each one.

Loo

Players: 5 to 8 (6 is best).

Cards: A regular pack of 52.

Equipment: A handful of counters—poker chips, matchsticks, toothpicks, dried beans, etc.

The Deal: Each player receives three cards, one at a time. An extra hand of three cards is dealt just to the left of the dealer. This is the *widow*. If the player to the left of the widow does not like her hand, she may throw it away and take the widow instead. If she is satisfied with her hand, though, she must say so and stick with it.

Then each player in turn has a chance to take the widow, until somebody takes it or all refuse it.

Give the same number of counters to each player.

The Play (Single Pool): After the matter of the widow is settled, the player to the left of the dealer makes the opening lead. You must always *follow suit* to the lead when you can; you must *play higher* than any other card in the trick, if you can. Later, once trump is declared and a plain suit is led of which you have none, you must *trump*, if you can.

The highest trump, or, if there is no trump, the highesy card of the suit led, wins the trick. Aces are high.

You must keep the tricks you have won face up on the table in front of you as you play.

Trumps: Play begins without any trump suit and continues that way so long as everybody follows suit to every lead. When somebody fails to follow suit, the top card of the undealt stock is turned over. This card decides the trump suit. The trick just played is examined and if a card that has been played turns out to be trump, that card wins the trick.

Scoring: To start a pool, the dealer must *ante up* three counters. When the pool contains no more than these three counters, it is a *single*, and play takes place as described above. After the play, the pool pays out one counter for each trick won. Players who have not won a trick must pay three counters into the next pool, making it a *double*—or jackpot.

Double Pool: This is formed by the dealer's ante of three plus any payments for *loo* (not winning a trick in the previous hand). After the deal, the next card of the deck is turned up, deciding the trump suit. After checking out their hands, the players must say in turn whether they will play or drop out. If all but the dealer drop out, he takes the pool. If only one player ahead of the dealer decides to play, the dealer must play, too. He may play for himself—in which case he cannot take the widow—or he may play to "defend the pool," in which case he must throw away his hand and take the widow. When the dealer plays merely to "defend the pool," he neither collects nor pays any counters; the pool settles with his opponent alone.

The nearest active player to the left of the dealer leads first. The other rules of play are the same as in a single pool.

The double pool pays out one-third of its contents for each trick won. A player who stays in and does not win a trick must pay three counters to the next pool.

To Win the Game: Win the largest number of counters.

Rams

Players: 3 to 5.

Cards: A pack of 32. Discard all 2s to 6s from a regular pack of 52. The cards rank:

(Highest)   (Lowest)

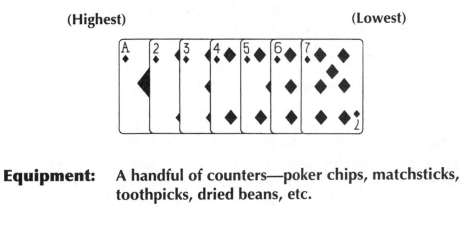

Equipment: A handful of counters—poker chips, matchsticks, toothpicks, dried beans, etc.

The Deal: Each player receives five cards in batches of three and two. An extra hand or *widow* is dealt, as in *Loo*. The last card belonging to the dealer is exposed to determine the trump suit.

Give the same number of counters to each player.

Declaring: After looking at their hands, the players in turn must declare whether they will play or drop out. If they play, they must undertake to win at least one trick. Any player in turn may discard the hand and take the widow instead (if it has not yet been taken).

Any player may declare *rams*—undertake to win *all* the tricks. This declaration may be made either before or after taking the widow, but it must be made before the next player has declared. In a *rams* game, everybody must play; players who have dropped out must pick up their hands again. If the rams player has not taken the widow, each player who has not refused it gets a chance to take it.

The Play: The player who declared rams makes the opening lead. Otherwise, it is made by the first player to the left of the dealer.

You must follow suit when you can, and you must play higher than any previous card in the trick, when you can. If a plain suit is led, you have to trump if you are able to, even if the trick has already been trumped. You must trump higher if you can. A trick is won by the highest trump in it, or, if no trump, by the highest card of the suit led.

Scoring: The dealer antes up five counters. The pool may contain counters left from the previous deal.

Each player who has stayed in the game takes one counter (or one-fifth of all the counters) from the pool for each trick he wins. Players (as in *Loo*) who win no tricks must pay five counters into the next pool.

In a rams, however, the settlement is different. If the rams player wins all the tricks, she wins the whole pool plus five counters from every other player. If she loses a trick, the cards are at once thrown in; she must pay enough counters to double the pool and five counters to every player.

If everybody ahead of the player to the right of the dealer passes, this player must pay the dealer five counters if he wishes to drop. In this case, the pool remains undivided. If only one player other than the dealer decides to play, the dealer must play to defend the pool. In this case, he takes the trump card and discards another face down.

Sixty-Six

Players: 2.

Cards: 24 cards: Ace, King, Queen, Jack, 10 and 9 of each suit. (Discard all 2s to 8s). The cards in each suit rank:

(Highest) (Lowest)

The Deal: Each player receives six cards, dealt three at a time. Place the rest of the pack face down in the middle of the table, to form the stock. Turn the top card of the stock face up and place it partly underneath the stock. This is the *trump card* and it decides the trump suit.

Early Play: The non-dealer leads first. The cards are played out in tricks. A trick is won by the higher trump or by the higher card played of the suit led. The winner of a trick draws the top card of the stock, and the opponent draws the next card. In this way, each hand is restored to six cards after each trick.

During this early play, you do not have to follow suit to the lead. You may play any card. The early play ends when the stock is exhausted.

To Win the Game: You try to meld marriages (see below), win cards in tricks and win the last trick. The first player to reach a total of 66 or more points wins a game point. The first one to score seven *game points* wins an overall game.

Marriages: A marriage is meld of a King and Queen of the same suit. In the trump suit, a marriage counts 40. In any other suit, it counts 20. To score a marriage, you must show it after winning a trick, then lead one of the two cards.

If the non-dealer wants to lead a King or Queen from a marriage for an opening lead, she may show the marriage and then do so. But she may not score the marriage until after she has won a trick.

Trump Card: A player who has the 9 of trumps may exchange it for the trump card—to get a higher trump. He may make this exchange only after winning a trick, before making the next lead.

Closing: At any turn to lead, a player may turn the trump card face down. By doing that he closes—that is, stops—any further drawing from the stock. The hands are played out as in *Later Play* (see below), except that marriages may still be melded.

Later Play: After the stock is exhausted, you play out the six cards in each hand. In this part of the game, you must follow suit to the lead, if you can.

Counting Cards: Cards won in tricks are counted as follows:

Each Ace	11
Each 10	10
Each King	4
Each Queen	3
Each Jack	2
For winning the last trick	10

Scoring: Marriages are scored on paper whenever melded. Points taken in tricks are not entered on paper until a hand is finished, but it is important to keep mental track of these points and your opponent's points as they are won. In your turn to play, you may claim thast you have reached 66. Then stop play at once and count. If you're right:

- **you score one *game point***
- **or two if your opponent has less than 33**
- **or three game points if he has not even won a trick.**

If you are wrong, and you don't have 66:

- **your opponent scores two game points**

The reason it's so important to realize when you have won a game—and to claim it—is that you may lose by playing out the hand. If you and your opponent both get more than 66, or if you tie at 65, neither of you wins. But the winner of the next hand gets one additional game point.

Usually, at least one game point is won by somebody in each deal. As mentioned earlier, you win by scoring seven game points in an overall game.

Three-Hand Sixty-Six

Players: 3.

Cards: Same as in *Sixty-Six*: 24 cards, Ace down to 9.

The Deal: The dealer gives six cards to the other two players, but deals none to himself.

The Play: The non-dealers play regular *Sixty-Six*.

Scoring: The dealer scores the same number of game points as the winner of the deal. If both players get 66 or more—or tie at 65 (without a claim—they score nothing and the dealer scores one. But a player is not allowed to win the overall game (seven points) when he is the dealer. If the usual scoring would put him up to seven points or over, his total becomes six, and he must win that last point as an active player.

Four-Hand Sixty-Six

Players: 4.

Cards: 32 cards from a regular pack. Ace, King, Queen, Jack, 10, 9, 8, and 7 of each suit. (Discard 2s through 6s.)

The Deal: Each player receives eight cards. The last card, turned face up for trump, is shown to each player, and then taken into the dealer's hand.

The Play: Players sitting opposite each other are partners. There is no melding. At all times you must follow suit to a lead, if possible, and also must, if possible, play higher than any card already played to the trick. When a plain suit is led and you have none, you must trump or overtrump if you can.

Scoring: Play out every hand. There is no advantage in claiming to have won. The winning side scores:

> **1 game point for having taken 66 to 99 or**
> **2 game points for 100 to 129 or**
> **3 game points for every trick (130).**

If the sides tie at 65, one extra game point goes to the side winning the next hand.

8
The Whist Family

Back in the 1890s the games editor of an English magazine received a letter to this effect:

"My son, aged nine, has seen his elders playing *Whist* and now wishes to learn the game. Can you recommend to me some simple game I can teach him that will serve as an introduction to *Whist?*"

The editor replied, "Yes, I can recommend such a game. The game is *Whist.*"

The fact is that the rules of Whist are simple and few. You can learn them in two minutes. Whist is just about the simplest of all card games to play *at*. What is not so easy is to play *Whist* well, for its extraordinary scope for skillful play lets the expert pull miles ahead of the beginner.

Whist

Players: 4, in partnerships.

Cards: Each receives 13 cards, dealt one at a time.
In every suit the cards rank:

(Highest)   **(Lowest)**

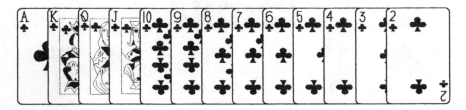

The Deal: The last card of the pack, belonging to the dealer, is exposed to all the players. This card decides the trump suit for that hand.

The Play: The player to the left of the dealer makes the first lead. The hands are played out in tricks. You must *follow suit* to the lead if possible. Otherwise, you may play or lead as you please. However, if a player *revokes* by not following suit when he has in his hand an appropriate card to play, he and his partner have to pay a penalty. The penalty is decided upon before play begins, and may be as severe as two game points for the opponent. The partnership cannot win any trick in which it revokes.

A trick is won by the highest trump in it, or, if it contains no trump, by the highest card of the suit led. The winner of a trick makes the lead for the next trick.

One member of each partnership gathers together all the tricks won by his side. He doesn't throw them together in a single pile but overlaps them crosswise, so that each batch of four cards remains separate from the others.

To Win the Game: Win as many tricks as possible. Points for tricks and honors are accumulated, and the first side to reach a total of seven game points wins.

Scoring: The side that wins the majority of the tricks scores

1 game point for each trick over 6, and, if agreed upon,
2 game points on the occasions when the opponents revoke.

In addition, points are scored for *honors*. The *honors* are the Ace, King, Queen and Jack of trumps.

If 2 honors were dealt to each side, there is no score.
If one side received 3 honors, it scores 2.
For all 4 honors, the score is 4.

Remember that honors are scored by the side to which they are *dealt*, not won in play. Both sides may score in the same deal, one side winning a majority of tricks and the other side holding a majority of honors.

Dummy Whist

Players: 3.

Cards: As in *Whist*.

The Deal: In this adaption of *Whist* for three players, four hands are dealt, as usual, with the extra hand or "dummy" going opposite the dealer.

The Play: The same as in *Whist*, except that the dealer plays the dummy hand as well as his own against the two live opponents. Of course, the dealer must be careful to play each hand at its proper turn.

Scoring: The dealer has a great advantage over his opponents, since he gets to see all 26 cards on his side. The fairest scoring method is to play three, six or nine deals so that each player has the same number of turns to deal. Then the player with the highest score is declared the winner.

Bridge Whist

This game is played in the same way as basic *Whist*, but it has a number of complications.

Players: 4, in partnerships.

Cards: Same as in *Whist*.

Equipment: Score pad and pencil.

Trumps: No trump card is turned. The dealer may name trump, if he wishes, or he may pass. If he does pass, his partner must name the trump. Any of the four suits may be named trump, or the player may call "No trump," meaning that the hand will be played without a trump suit.

Doubles: After the trump—or no trump—is named, either one of the non-dealers may declare "I double." This multiplies the score of the winners by two.

After such a double, either member of the dealer's side may declare "I re-double" or "I double back." The terms may re-double alternately without limit, until one team quits. Then the cards are played.

The Play: After the opening lead by the player to the left of the dealer, the dealer's partner puts her cards face up on the table in vertical rows by suit. The dealer then plays the "dummy" as well as his own hand, just as in *Dummy Whist.*

Scoring: The score is kept on a score pad. The sheet is divided into two halves by a vertical line. All the scores for one team (WE) are entered in the left-hand column, and the scores of the other team (THEY) in the right. The sheet is also divided by a horizontal line, somewhat below the middle. Only odd trick scores are entered below the line, and they are accumulated to determine when a game has been won (total score of 30).

All other scores go above the line. When the play ends, each column is added up to determine the grand total won by each side, for odd tricks, honors, slams, rubbers. For instance, the score sheet may look like this:

	WE	THEY
Honors & Bonuses →	40 20 100	
Tricks →		
Game 1 →	30	24
Game 2 → = A Rubber	120	

Scoring Tricks: The team winning at least six of the 13 tricks has a "book." It will score only tricks in excess of books of six. These scoreable tricks are called *odd tricks*. Score them as follows:

If trumps were	♠	♣	♦	♥	No trump
Each odd trick would count	2	4	6	8	10

Each double that was made multiplies the score of the winners by two, each redouble by four.

Scoring Honors: Points are also scored for honors, which are written above the line on your score sheet. These are kept separate from points for tricks, which are written below the line.

The honor count is considerably more complicated than in *Whist*. When the game is played in a trump suit, the five top trumps—Ace, King, Queen, Jack and 10—become honors. You take the odd-trick value and multiply it by the number shown below to get the honor score, which gets written above the line.

Team with 3 honors or *chicane*	**X 2**
(chicane is a hand without a trump)	
4 honors divided between partners	**X 4**
4 honors in one hand	**X 8**
4 honors in one hand, 5th in partner's	**X 9**
5 honors in one hand	**X 10**

When you multiply this out, remember that the score you get is for honors only. It does not affect the scoring of the odd tricks, which you have already written below the line.

In a no-trump game, the honors are the four Aces. Score them as follows:

Team with 3 Aces	**30**
4 Aces, divided	**40**
4 Aces in one hand	**100**

Scoring Bonuses: If one side wins all 13 tricks, it scores a bonus of 40 for *grand slam*. For winning 12 tricks, a *little slam*, there is a bonus of 20. These numbers get written above the line on your score pad.

To Win the Game: The first team to win 30 points in odd tricks wins a game. The team to win a *rubber*—two games—wins a bonus of 100 points, and *the* game.

Nullo Games

In order to win nullo games, you need to *avoid* winning tricks, or avoid taking certin cards in tricks. Most of the games are especially easy for children to learn because they have practically no other rules. Only in *Omnibus Hearts* do we find the added wrinkle that you *do* want to win some cards while you *don't* want to win others.

Four Jacks

Other Name: Polignac

Players: 4, 5, or 6.

Cards: With 4 players, 32 cards as follows: Ace, King, Queen, Jack, 10, 9, 8, 7—a full deck, but with all 2s to 6s discarded. All the 32 cards are dealt; each player receives 8 cards.

With 5 or 6 players, 30 cards—same as above but the two black 7s are also discarded. Each player receives 6 or 5 cards.

Equipment: A handful of counters—poker chips, matchsticks, dried beans, etc. Distribute the same number to each player.

The Play: The player to the left of the dealer leads first. The hands are played out in tricks. There is no trump suit. Each trick is won by the highest card played of the suit led.

To Win the Game: Avoid winning any Jacks. But before the opening lead, any player may announce that he will try to win all the tricks. This is called *capot*.

Scoring: Payments for holding Jacks and winning capot are made into a common pool, which is divided equally among all the players when the game ends. Whenever one player is down to his last counter, all players take equal numbers of counters from the pool.

If capot is announced and made, every player must pay five counters. But if the capot player fails to win all the tricks, he alone pays five counters.

When capot is not announced, the player who takes the Jack of Spades—called Polignac—must pay two counters into the pool. One counter must be paid for each of the other three Jacks taken in.

Slobberhannes

This game is played in much the same way as *Four Jacks*, with the difference that what you want to avoid winning are:

first trick
last trick
the Queen of Clubs

Each of these costs one counter, and if you unluckily take all three, you must pay an extra counter—four in all.

9
The Hearts Family

This is the chief group of nullo games. In all of them, the way to win is to avoid winning Hearts.

If you are invited to play *Hearts* with a group that you have never played with before, it's a good idea to ask them to state the rules. Otherwise, you may find yourself playing one game while they play another.

The name of the basic game, *Hearts*, is used loosely for all its offspring, but there are many variations. *Black Maria* and *Black Lady* often denote games that are different from either the *Black Lady* or *Hearts* described here.

Hearts

This is the basic and most simple game of the *Hearts* family, though the most popular is *Black Lady*.

Players: 2 to 6, but almost always 4. Other forms of the game are preferred with more or less than 4.

Cards: Each player receives 13 cards. When you can't divide the cards equally, remove enough deuces from the deck to make the deal come out even. Aces rank highest.

Equipment: A handful of counters—poker chips, matchsticks, toothpicks, dried beans, etc.—the same amount to each player—or pencil and paper.

To Win the Game: Avoid winning any Hearts—or win all 13 of them.

The Play: The player to the left of the dealer makes an opening lead and the cards are played in tricks. A trick is won by the highest card played of the suit led. There is no trump suit, though Hearts are often mistakenly called "trumps." The winner of a trick leads to the next trick.

Scoring with counters: For each Heart that a player wins, he must pay one counter into the pool.

If two or more players took no Hearts, they divide the pool.

But if all players took Hearts, nobody wins the pool. It stays on the table as a *jackpot* and becomes part of the pool for the next deal.

Scoring with pencil and paper: Each Heart taken counts one point against the player. A game can be ended at any agreed-upon time, and the player with the lowest total score is the winner. The usual method is to charge a player 13 if he wins all the Hearts. A good alternative is to deduct 13—(or 26, as agreed) from his score, preserving the principle that a player with a bad hand should have a chance to save himself (or gain) by taking *all* the Hearts.

Heartsette

This game adapts *Hearts* to an odd number of players.

Players: 3 or 5.

Cards: Place a *widow* (a group of cards) on the table—
4 cards if 3 are playing, 2 cards if 5 are playing.

The Deal: Deal out the rest of the cards.

The Play: Play in the same way as *Hearts*, but the widow is turned
face up after the first trick and goes to the winner of that trick. He must
of course pay for any Hearts it contains.

Spot Hearts

This variation features a different scoring method that you can apply to
any member of the Hearts family. The charges for taking Hearts go according to rank:

Ace counts	14
King counts	13
Queen counts	12
Jack counts	11
Others count	face value

Joker Hearts

This is *Hearts*, with a Joker added.

Players: Same.

Cards: **Add a Joker to the pack, discarding the 2 of Clubs to keep the deck at 52 cards.**

The Joker can be beaten only by the Ace, King, Queen or Jack of Hearts. Otherwise, it wins any trick to which it is played.

   If you're playing *Heartsette*, deal an extra card to the widow.

   The Joker counts as one Heart in payment or, in *Spot Hearts* scoring, 20.

Draw Hearts

This is *Hearts* for two players.

Players: 2.

Cards: **13 to each player.**

The Deal: Place the rest of the deck face down in the middle of the table, forming the stock.

To Win the Game: Take fewer Hearts.

The Play: The cards are played in tricks. The winner of a trick draws the top card of the stock, and his opponent takes the next. After the stock is exhausted, the hands are played out without drawing.

Auction Hearts

The idea of this game is to let the players bid for the privilege of naming the suit to be avoided.

Each player in turn has one chance to bid, and the highest bidder names the "minus" suit.

Bids are made in numbers of counters that the player is willing to pay into the pool. Settlement is also made with counters, as in basic *Hearts*.

If the pool becomes a jackpot, there is no bidding in the next deal. The same player retains the right to name the minus suit, without further payment, until the jackpot is won. This player also makes the opening lead.

Domino Hearts

Players: 5 or 6.

Cards: Each receives 6 cards.

The Deal: The rest of the pack is put face down in the middle of the table, forming the stock. All tricks must be composed of cards of the same suit—there is no discarding. When a player is unable to follow suit to the lead, he must draw from the stock until he gets a playable card. After the stock is exhausted, he must pass.

When a player's hand is exhausted, he drops out of the deal and the others play on. If he should win a trick with his last card, the player to his left leads for the next trick.

When all but one have dropped out, the last player must add his remaining cards to his own tricks.

Hearts taken are charged at one point each.

To Win the Game: Have the lowest total when another player reaches 31 points.

Black Lady

This is the best-known game of the *Hearts* family. It is what most people refer to when they speak of *Hearts*.

Players: 3 to 7. It is best for 4, without partnerships.

Cards: Deal out the whole pack, giving equal hands to all.
With 4 players it works out correctly.
With 3 players, discard 1 deuce.
With 5 players, discard 2 deuces.
With 6 players, discard 4 deuces.
With 7 players, discard 3 deuces.

Equipment: A handful of counters—poker chips, matchsticks, toothpicks, dried beans, etc.—the same amount to each player or: Pencil and paper for scoring.

The Pass: After looking at his hand, each player passes any three cards he chooses to the player to his left. He must choose which cards he is going to pass and put them on the table before picking up the three cards passed to him by the player to his right.

The Play: The player to the left of the dealer makes the opening lead. The cards are played out in tricks. Aces rank highest. A trick is won by the highest card played of the suit led. The winner of a trick leads to the next trick.

To Win the Game: Avoid taking the Queen of Spades—called Black Lady, Black Maria, Calamity Jane, etc.—and avoid taking Hearts; or else take *all* the Hearts *and* the Queen of Spades, called "shooting the moon."

Scoring: If one player takes all 14 "minus" cards, he can subtract 26 points from his score. Some people play instead that 26 points are added to everyone else's score. Otherwise, one point is charged for each Heart won, and 13 points for the Queen of Spades. A running total score is kept for each player on paper. The first one to reach 100 or more loses the game, and the one with the lowest total at that time wins.

When playing with young children, you may want a shorter game. In this case, set the limit at 50.

An alternative method is to score with counters, settling after each hand. Payments are made into a pool, distributed equally to the players from time to time.

Strategy: See *Omnibus Hearts* (pages 102-103).

Cancellation Hearts

This is a variation for 6 or more players.

Players: 6 or more.

Cards: 2 packs shuffled together.

The Deal: Deal the cards as far as they will go evenly. Put the extra cards face down on the table as a widow. This group of cards goes to the winner of the first trick.

The Play: You play the game exactly the same way as *Black Lady*, except:

1. When two identical cards, such as two Aces of Diamonds, are played in the same trick, they cancel each other out, ranking as zero. They cannot win the trick. As a result, if a deuce is led and all the higher cards of the suit played to a trick are paired and therefore cancelled, the deuce would win the trick!

2. When all cards of the suit led are cancelled, the cards stay on the table and go to the next winner of a trick. The same leader leads again.

Scoring: As in *Black Lady*. Counters make for easier scoring than paper and pencil.

Discard Hearts

This is *Black Lady*, except that the three cards are sometimes passed to the left and sometimes to the right. The best plan is to alternate. The pass often allows you to ruin your neighbor. Alternate passing gives her the chance to get back at you.

Omnibus Hearts

Many players regard this as the most interesting game of the Hearts family. It is the same as *Black Lady* with one addition. The Jack of Diamonds, or sometimes the 10, is a "plus" card, counting 10 *for* you if you win it.

As a result, in this game, each suit has its own character: Clubs are neutral, Diamonds contain the plus card, Spades contain the worst minus card, and all the Hearts are minus cards. A player who makes a "take-all" must win all 13 Hearts, the Queen of Spades and the Jack of Diamonds.

Strategy: The most dangerous cards to hold are high Spades—Ace, King, Queen—without enough lower cards to guard them. Pass such high Spades when you are dealt less than three lower Spades. Pass high Hearts if you can afford to, and if they look dangerous, but two *low* Hearts are usually enough to guard them. Any suit outside of Spades is dangerous if you have four or more without any card lower than, say, a six. Even a single very low card—a two or a three—may not be a sufficient guard. Pass one to three cards from the top or middle of such a suit, if you do not have more pressing troubles.

If you do not have any high Spades after the pass, lead Spades at every opportunity. You can never gather Black Maria by a lower Spade lead! You want to try to force her out by Spade leads so that you can save yourself from winning her by discard. If you have her yourself, it is usually best to lead your shortest side suit so as to get rid of it and get a chance to discard Black Maria.

If you are dealt the Jack of Diamonds, pass it if you can afford to. The Jack is musch easier to *catch* than to *save*. It is not often caught by higher Diamonds—and when it is, it is mostly by accident. It usually falls to the winner of the last trick. The hand with which you may hope to catch it has some Aces and Kings, adequately guarded by lower cards, in two or more suits. Of Course, if you hope to catch the Jack, don't pass any higher Diamonds, and don't ever lead Diamonds if you can avoid it. But put a *high* Diamond on any Diamond lead that might be won by the Jack if you were to play low.

Don't attempt a take-all without a very powerful hand. Certain holdings are fatal no matter how strong you are in other suits—low Hearts, for example (not at the end of a long solid suit), and the Jack of Diamonds (without enough Diamond length and strength to save the Jack even if you do not go for take-all). However, if you've got one or two middling-high Hearts, it is not fatal. You may be able to win the tricks simply by leading these Hearts. The players holding higher Hearts may shrink away from taking the tricks.

When your chief ambition is to avoid taking minus cards, which is most of the time, get rid of your high cards early rather than late. Thus, if you have:

put the Ace on the *first* Club and the Jack on the *second*, saving your 2 to escape having to win the more dangerous third lead. The more often a suit is led, the more likely it becomes that Black Maria or Hearts will be discarded on it.

SECTION 2

10 Minute
Card Games

Introduction

I have long enjoyed playing card games because they have provided me, my family, and friends with wholesome entertainment, camaraderie, and deeper, richer, more meaningful relationships through friendly competition. Hoping, then, to share these benefits with my readers, I have prepared this section of ten-minute card games.

Why titled *Ten-Minute Card Games?* Simply to remind the reader that most card games require only ten minutes or less to play, and that you do not need large blocks of time for a game once you have learned the rules. Probably all basic card games at first required ten minutes or less to play, but some became more complicated and required longer periods of play in response to players' wanting to prolong the game. For example, over a period of time, *Bridge* evolved from *Whist, Black Lady* from the simpler game of *Hearts,* and a host of other cards games from a few basic parent games such as *Seven-Up, Rummy, Straight Poker,* and others.

My first goal in preparing this section was to offer card games that began as and remained ten minute games, as well as those that began as ten minute games but were lengthened somewhat by advanced scoring procedures. In the latter case, I simplified the scoring to return these games to a one-hand, one-game format. However, in each such case I also included the scoring procedure for the higher-score, longer-lasting game for those persons who want to play it.

My second goal was to address both men and women, partly because both play cards, and partly out of a sense of fairness. With this goal in mind, I have used both feminine and masculine pronouns throughout the text.

—William A. Moss

The All Fours Group

Card players have enjoyed games of the All Fours group, including Seven-Up and its many variations, since the late 1600s. Having its origins in England, Seven-Up, along with Whist and Put, was popular in the early 1700s and for years competed with Poker as the favorite gambling game in the United States.

Seven-Up

Players and Deck Used: The game requires two, three, or four persons (when they are playing as partners, two against two) and a full deck of 52 cards. The cards rank as follows:

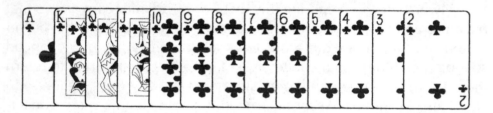

Beginning the Game: The players cut for high card to determine the first deal and partners (when four play). Highest cut becomes the dealer, and high cuts play as partners against low cuts. After the shuffle and cut, the dealer gives six cards to each player, three at a time, in rotation from left to right. After completing the deal, the dealer faces, or turns up, the next card to show the "trump" suit, any card of which will win over any card of another suit. If the card turned up is a Jack, the dealer scores 1 point. If more than two persons are playing, only the dealer and first player can look at their hands until the turned-up card is accepted or rejected as trump. The deal passes to the left at the end of each hand.

The Goals: The goals of the game are: (a) to hold the highest and lowest trumps in play; (b) to turn the Jack for trumps or to capture it in play; and (c) to capture cards in play that count towards game.

Making the Trump: The player seated to the dealer's left has the first right to *stand* or *beg*. If she is satisfied with the trump turned, she "stands" and leads (plays the first card) to the first *trick* (sequence of cards played). If she *begs*, the dealer must either say "Take it" and give her a 1-point *gift* to let the trump stand, or deal three new cards to each player and turn up a new trump. The dealer, however, cannot give her the 1-point gift if it will give her "game" (winning) point. If the dealer chooses to give each player three more cards and turns up a trump that is the same as the first one, the dealer then repeats the process until she turns up a card of a different suit. This process is called *running the deck*. If she turns up the Jack of the rejected trump suit while running the deck, she does not score 1 point for doing so. If a new trump is turned up while running the deck, all players keep their best six cards, discarding the others. However, if the dealer runs the whole deck without turning up a different trump, she collects the cards and redeals.

The Play: The player seated to the dealer's left leads any card. If the card is a trump, the players must follow suit, if possible. If the card is not a trump, the players must follow suit, but, if unable to do so, they may either play a trump or discard. The highest card in the suit led wins, unless the trick is "trumped," in which case the highest trump wins. The winner of each trick leads to the next trick.

Scoring: The players score points as follows:
  High— the highest trump in play. Player to whom dealt gets 1 point.
  Low— the lowest trump in play. Player to whom dealt gets 1 point.
  Jack— Jack of trumps. If in play, scored by the dealer turning it up as trump or by the player taking it in a trick: 1 point.
  Game—won by person holding cards with the highest point count taken during play: 1 point

In counting points for game, 10s count as 10 points; Aces, 4; Kings, 3; Queens, 2; Jacks; 1. If there is a tie for "game" between the dealer and a nondealer, the latter wins; otherwise, no one scores game point. If a player holds the only trump in play, she will win high and low, and, if the card she holds is the trump Jack, she will win high, low, and Jack.

Game: The player taking the greatest number of points in one hand wins the game. Many Seven-Up enthusiasts, however, prefer playing successive hands, usually two to three, until one of the players scores 7 or 10 points, as agreed to at the beginning of the game. In the latter procedure, the first player to score 7 (or 10) points wins the game. For example, if the dealer needs 1 point to "go out" and she turns the Jack of trumps, she wins. If both players take enough points to win the game in the same hand, they score their points in this order: high, low, Jack, and game.

Remedies and Penalties: If a player intentionally or unintentionally exposes a card, she places it face up on the table and plays it when it is legal to do so. If all players agree, they may allow the offender to keep the card in her hand during the play.

A player who revokes, or fails to follow suit when she could have done so, incurs penalties if she does not correct the revoke before the trick is *quitted* (placed face down) and the next lead made. If she does not correct the revoke, she cannot "go out" in that hand, nor can she cumulatively score more than 6 points. Additionally, if the trump Jack is not in play, she forfeits 1 point of her score; if the trump Jack is in play, she forfeits 2 points.

Many players prefer a stiffer penalty for a revoke, such as forfeiture of the game.

Variation: If a player begs in a three-hand game and the dealer decides to give her 1 point instead of running the deck, she must also give 1 point to the other nondealer. If the first player in a three-hand game *stands*, the next player has the right to stand or beg. If both stand, the first player leads to the first trick.

Auction Pitch, or Setback

Auction Pitch is basically the same game as Seven-Up with the following exceptions:

1. Two to seven players usually play *cutthroat*—each for himself. Partnership play is optional.

2. After dealing six cards to each person, three at a time, the trump suit is not decided by the dealer turning it up: instead, the players bid to name the trump suit.

3. The player seated to the left of the dealer opens the bidding. He may pass or bid from 1 to 4 points. If he bids 4 points, which is the maximum bid, he *pitches*, or leads, his trump suit immediately. If he bids less than 4 points, each player in rotation to the left may pass or bid at least 1 point more than the previous bid until a 4-point bid is made or until each player has had one opportunity to bid. Each player bases his bid on the number of points (high, low, Jack, and game) he thinks he can take in play. The high bidder opens the play by pitching the trump of his choice. If he accidently pitches the wrong card, the card pitched remains the trump card. If any player, intentionally or unintentionally, piches a card during the bidding process, he assumes the burden of a 4-point bid.

4. If the high bidder makes his bid, he wins the hand and the game. However, as discussed above in Seven-Up, many players prefer playing until one of them scores 7 or 10 points, as agreed to at the beginning of the game. In this instance, the first person to score 7 (or 10) points wins the game, unless, of course, the pitcher (high bidder) also goes out in the same hand. In the latter case, the pitcher wins.

5. If, in playing the 7- or 10-point game, a pitcher fails to make his bid, he is set back the amount of his bid, and he subtracts that amount from his score. If he is set back more points than he has, he is said to be *in the hole*, and his score is circled or preceded by a minus sign.

6. If a player other than the pitcher revokes, the pitcher cannot be set back, and each nonoffending player scores what he makes. The revoking player, however, is set back the amount of the bid. If the pitcher revokes, he cannot score any points; instead, he is set back the amount of his bid, and the other players score what they make.

Other than the above differences, Auction Pitch and Seven-Up are the same game.

Variations: Many players like to include the jick (same color Jack as trump Jack) and joker in their pitch games. When they do, the Jick and Joker each are worth 1 point, and high cards rank as follows: Ace (high), King, Queen, Jack, Jick, Joker, and 10. The Jick and Joker also count 1 point in determining the winner of game point. If the players use the Jick and Joker, they should adjust the high bid and game score accordingly, usually 6 and 10 points, respectively.

Straight Pitch

Straight pitch differs from Auction Pitch in the following respects:

　　1. After the dealer gives each player six cards, three at a time, she turns the top card of the stock to name the trump suit. There is no bidding.

　　2. The player sitting to the dealer's left leads to the first trick. The winner of each trick leads to the next trick.

　　3. The inclusion of the Jick and Joker in the game is common.

Ranking of Cards in Straight Pitch

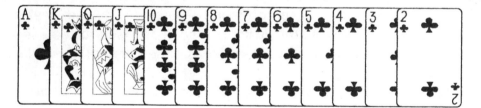

The Poker Group

Poker evolved slowly from an old French game called *Gilet*, which in turn probably had its origins in the Italian game of *Primero*. During the reign of Charles IX (1560-1574), notable for its bloody civil wars between the Catholics and Huguenot Protestants, *Gilet* became the game of *Brelan*. By the time of the French Revolution, the game of *Brelan* developed into *Bouillotte*, which included such devices as the blind, freeze-out, raise, bluff, and table stakes—all of which are common to modern-day Poker.

Bouillotte also gave rise to *Ambigu*, which supplied the draw, and the English game of *Brag*, which was largely a bluffer's game. These three games—*Bouillotte, Ambigu,* and *Brag*—shaped modern-day Poker, along with the adoption of the 52-card deck by 1835 and the introduction of five, instead of three, dealt cards.

Basic Poker

Two to eight persons play Poker with a 52-card deck. The players sometimes limit the number of people allowed to participate according to the game being played and the number of cards needed to fill out the hands. A joker may be added to the deck by mutual consent, and, if the joker is added, it is wild and is used as the holder wishes. The cards rank: 2 (low) to Ace (high). But sometimes at the beginning of a game, the players agree to an Ace's being used as high *or* low, such as in low sequences, or runs.

Seating: Players usually sit where they please, but some prefer to determine the seating arrangement by dealing each person one card face up, letting the person with low sit to the dealer's left, next low to his left, and so forth. Ties are broken by cutting for low card. The players may decide where a newcomer sits by mutual agreement, by the method above, or by some other means of choice.

Chips: By mutual consent, one player assumes the role of banker and takes charge of exchanging chips for money and for settling accounts at the end of the card session. (Matchsticks, beans, etc. may be substituted for chips.) Again by mutual consent, the players decide on the value of white, red, blue, and yellow chips.

Before the Game Begins: Poker players should decide the following at the start of the game: (a) the amount of the ante (preliminary bet made before the deal), as well as who antes (sometimes the dealer only, but usually all players); (b) a bet/raise limit; and (c) a time set to stop the card session. Instead of setting a time to end a session, some players prefer playing *freeze-out*. In freeze-out, all players begin the card session with the same number of chips, and as soon as any player loses his chips, he retires from the session, which continues until one player has won all the chips. Sometimes the players also set a limit to the number of times that a bet may be raised, which oftentimes is three raises, or *bumps*.

Beginning the Game: Players customarily determine the first dealer by having the cards dealt around face up, one at a time, until a Jack falls—the person who receives the first Jack deals. (Some players prefer to draw or cut for high or low card to determine the first dealer.) Before the cards are actually dealt, the dealer and, sometimes, the other players, depending on the game being played, ante chips on the middle of the table to begin the "pot."

The shuffle and cut are as in other card games. However, the person sitting to the dealer's right may decline to cut the deck. If he does decline, the players to his right, in turn, may cut or decline to do so. If all players decline, the deal proceeds. The dealer gives each player his cards, one at a time, in clockwise rotation, beginning with the person to his left. (This applies to *all* Poker games.) The dealer cannot deal the last card; instead, he shuffles this card with the discards to rebuild his dealing stock.

The Stripped Deck: If there are only three or four people playing, they may choose to strip the deck of its 2s, 3s, and, sometimes, 4s. If the players strip the deck and Aces are low, an 8-high straight would consist of: 8, 7, 6, 5, and Ace.

The Goal: The goal of each round of Poker is to hold or draw to the best hand, thereby winning the pot or a portion of it, depending on the game being played. In determining the winner(s) of each pot, the custom among poker players is to "let the cards speak for themselves."

Poker hands rank from high to low as follows:

1. Five of a kind. Five cards of the same rank, or denomination, which is possible only when the joker is included in the deck and/or other wild cards are named.

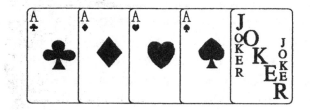

2. Royal straight flush. An Ace, King, Queen, Jack, and 10 squence, or run, in any suit.

3. Straight flush. A five-card sequence, or run, in any suit ranked by its highest card. For example, a player would call his club sequence of 10, 9, 8, 7, and 6 a straight flush, 10 high. A 10-high straight flush would rank over a 9-high straight flush.

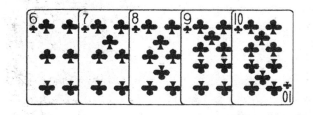

115

4. Four of a kind, which is ranked by its denomination. For example, four Queens rank over four Jacks.

5. Full house. A combination of three cards of one denomination and two cards of another: for example, three Kings and two 10s. The "triplet" (three of a kind) decides rank. For example, three Kings and two 10s rank over three Queens and two Jacks (or three Kings rank over three Queens).

6. Flush. Any five cards in a suit, but not in sequence. A player ranks a flush by the highest card in the flush.

7. Straight. A sequence, or run, of five cards in various suits, which is ranked by its highest card.

8. Three of a kind, or three cards of the same denomination, which are ranked by their denomination.

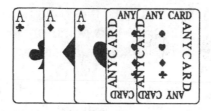

9. Two pairs of any denominations, which are ranked by the highest pair. For example, Jacks and 5s would rank over 10s and 8s.

10. One pair of any denomination with three unmatched cards. A pair is ranked by denomination.

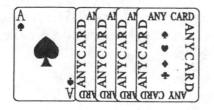

11. High card. A hand with none of the combinations listed above ranked by its highest card. In case of a tie, the player holding a card of the next higher denomination wins.

Ties: If the high cards in flushes tie, the next higher cards determine the winner. Ties in straight flushes, full houses, flushes, and straights divide the pot. In dividing such pots, the players usually cut for high card to determine the ownership of odd chips. If players hold four of a kind, a full house (in a seven-card game), two pairs, or one pair tie, their unmatched cards break the tie by rank. If high cards tie, the other cards again break the tie by rank.

Note: In cases where one or two tying hands has a Joker, many players hold that the natural hand, the one without the joker, wins. Other players hold the opposite view, because the odds of drawing a Joker are less than drawing a natural hand. But the latter group also holds that if both tying hands have multiple wild cards, the one with the fewer wild cards wins. *If a poker group wants to break ties involving wild cards by one of the methods just discussed, they should mutually agree to the method at the start of the game to avoid disputes and, perhaps, hard feelings.* Otherwise, tied hands split the pot according to guidelines set forth in the paragraph above.

Table Stakes: While a hand is in progress, a player may, with the consent of the other players, raise the betting limit to *table stakes*, which is the amount of chips he has on the table at the time. No one can raise the amount of the table stakes after looking at any of his cards. If another player does not have enough chips to *call*, or *see*, the table stakes raise, he may call a *sight* of the last bettor's cards for what chips he does have and separate that part of the pot from the rest.

The other players continue their calls and raises; some of these players also may call for a sight and thus fragment the pot further. If the person calling for a sight holds the winning hand during the showdown, he wins only that part of the pot for which he called his sight; the other players decide on the winner of the rest of the pot on the merits of their respective hands.

An accelerated variation of table stakes is the double-up game, wherein each player to the left of the dealer may in turn call for table stakes raises that would stop at a previously agreed-to number of such raises—usually up to six.

Remedies and Penalties: In case of a misdeal, the dealer deals again with the same pack. If a card is exposed in cutting or in reuniting a pack, the dealer must shuffle the deck again and redeal. Other misdeals include; an uncut or improperly reunited deck; a card placed face up in the deck; an incomplete or otherwise imperfect deck. If an extra but unexposed card is accidently given to a player, the dealer can restore it to the top of the deck or continue his deal with it, whichever action is more appropriate.

If a player has a hand of fewer or more than the cards needed for the game, if he has looked at them, and if he has bet on them, his hand is foul. He then must, upon discovery, abandon the hand, forfeiting the chips he has put into the pot and even the pot itself if he won it on that deal. If a player finds that he has too many or too few cards and he has not looked at them, he may request that the dealer remedy the card count by drawing cards from his hand or by dealing additional cards to his hand to leave it at the correct number of cards. However, if more than one hand is irregular in the deal and cannot be easily remedied, the cards must be shuffled, cut, and dealt again.

If a player has looked at any of his cards, he cannot ask for a new deal unless the deck is found to be imperfect. A deal out of turn or with the wrong deck must be stopped before it is completed; otherwise it stands.

If a player bets, calls, and/or raises out of sequence, the turn returns to the appropriate player. However, any chips the offender put in the pot remain there, and when his turn comes around, his bet, call, or raise is regarded as already made. In effect, he can make no further bets or raises until his turn comes around again, if it does. If he owes chips in addition to those put in the pot earlier, he makes up the difference. If he put too many chips in the pot, he forfeits them to the pot.

If a player announces a bet, call, or raise out of turn but does not put the chips in the pot, his announcement is void and the turn to bet, call, or raise reverts to the appropriate player.

If any player puts more chips in the pot than are required by a bet, call, or raise, he forfeits the excess chips to the pot. If he puts too few chips in the pot, he must make up the difference.

Straight, or Bluff, Poker

Straight Poker, the immediate forerunner of all modern-day poker games, at first required four players and a 20-card deck (Aces, Kings, Queens, Jacks, and 10s), with each person being dealt a five-card hand. Although the original game is still a popular two-hand game, it is now more often played by two to eight persons with a 52-card deck.

In Straight Poker, only the dealer antes. After she has done so and the cards are shuffled and cut, she gives each player five cards face down, one at a time, and in clockwise rotation. Beginning with the player at the dealer's left, each person, in turn, may drop from the game, check (put the lowest value of chips in the pot to remain in the game), or make a bet, placing her chips in the middle of the table. Once a bet is made, the other players remaining in the game must either call the bet or drop out of the game. A player calling a bet may also raise it, which requires the other players to call the raise if they want to stay in the game. During this round of betting and raising, a player holding a weak hand might try to bluff the others out of the game by betting and/or raising excessively, hoping thereby "to buy" the pot. If no one *sees* the bet (meets or equals it), the bettor wins the pot without having to show her cards. If the bet or bet and raises are called, all players still in the game expose their hands face up for the showdown. The best poker hand wins the pot.

Draw Poker

In Draw Poker each player antes, and the dealer gives each person five cards face down, one at a time, and in clockwise rotation. After receiving and examining his cards, each player, beginning with the one at the dealer's left, drops from the game, bets, or checks the bet of the person at his left. After all players pass or after all bets and raises have been called, each player discards his unwanted cards face down, and the dealer gives him replacements.

After the players examine the cards they received on the draw, a second round of betting takes place. Following this second betting interval, the players lay their cards face up on the table for the show-down. The person holding the best hand wins.

Variations of Draw Poker: A player may open the betting without holding a pair. However, many players prefer playing a variation of Draw Poker called *Jacks or Better*, or *Jackpots*. In this variation, a player must hold a pair of Jacks or a hand better than Jacks in order to open the betting. In this variation, if no one can open the betting, everyone antes another chip to the pot and the cards are gathered up, shuffled, cut, and dealt again. If a person opens the betting and is later discovered to not have held the requisite cards to open, he must pay a penalty, which usually is double the size of the final pot.

Another variation of Draw Poker is *Progressive Draw Poker,* wherein a player needs Jacks or better to open the betting. If no one can open with Jacks or better, everyone antes another chip to the pot while the cards are gathered up, shuffled, cut, and dealt again. On the second deal, a player must have Queens or better to open the betting—hence the title Progressive Draw Poker. If no one can open with Queens or better, the third deal requires Kings or better; the fourth deal requires Aces or better; the fifth deal returns to Jacks or better; and so forth. Players like this variation because it builds large pots quickly.

Another popular variation is *Pass and Out*, wherein a player may open the betting holding nothing more than a pair, but in each turn he must either bet or drop out. He cannot "pass," or check, the betting to the next player.

Draw Poker with a Joker: While playing Draw Poker, as well as some other games, some players like to include the Joker, or *bug*, in the deck. The Joker affects the game as follows:

1. The person holding the Joker may use it as any card she wishes with one exception: She cannot use the Joker in a flush to replace a card she already holds. For example, she cannot use it as an Ace with an Ace-high flush and call that flush a double-Ace-high flush or straight flush. Nonetheless, the Joker makes it possible for a player to hold as many as five of a kind, which ranks over all other hands.

2. For showdown purposes, if two hands are equal in all respects, the tied hands split the pot, unless the players agree at the start of the game that a natural hand ranks over one with a Joker or other wild cards.

Deuces Wild

Deuces (twos) Wild is another variation of Draw Poker with a Joker. Deuces affect the game as follows:

    1. Each deuce, or 2, ranks as a Joker and may be used as any card its holder wishes, except the duplicate of a card he already holds in a flush, as explained in Poker with a Joker. The players also may wish to include the Joker in a Deuces Wild game.

    2. For showdown purposes, tied hands split the pot, unless the players agree at the start of the game that the hand with no or the fewest wild cards breaks such ties.

Wild Widow

Wild Widow is a variation of Draw Poker. The two games differ as follows:

    1. The dealer gives the players four cards one at a time face down, turns the next card face up as the Wild Widow in the middle of the table, and then deals one more card face down to each person.

    2. If a player holds a card or cards that match the face-up Wild Widow (the designated wild card), she may call and use them in any way she chooses, as in Deuces Wild. The players also may include the Joker in the deck.

Spit in the Ocean

Spit in the Ocean is another variation of Draw Poker. The two games differ as follows:

    1. The dealer gives each player four cards face down and then turns the next card, which is wild, face up in the middle of the table.

    2. If a player holds a card or cards that match the face-up card, he may call and use them in any way he chooses, as in Deuces Wild.

    3. Each player regards the face-up card as the fifth card of his hand, and he bases his draw on four cards only.

Lowball

Lowball is a variation of Draw Poker, in which the lowest-ranking hand, rather than the highest -ranking, wins the pot. There are no minimum requirements to open the pot, and straights and flushes do not count. In Lowball, Aces are always low; hence a pair of Aces ranks lower than a pair of deuces, and the lowest hand possible is a 5, 4, 3, 2, and Ace, whether it is made up of one or two suits.

During play, a player may check, or pass. If no one bets and the dealer has called for bets twice, a showdown takes place and the lowest hand wins the ante.

Ranking of Cards in Lowball

Lowest Hand of Any Suit or Combination of Suits

Five-Card Stud

Typically, there is no ante in a Stud game, unless one has been agreed to by the players. If one player antes, all ante. After the shuffle and cut, the dealer gives each person one card face down (the hole card), then one card face up, in clockwise rotation. In Five- and Seven-Card Stud, the dealer customarily announces the first bettor in each betting interval by pointing out the high card or best face-up hand. He likewise points out possible hands, such as possible straights, flushes, and so forth.

The players examine their face-down cards, and the person

receiving the highest face-up card must open the betting or drop from the game. In the case of a tie for high card, the person receiving the first high card bets. If this person drops from the game, the person with the next highest card bets, and a betting interval follows.

After the first round of betting is completed, the dealer then gives each player still in the game a second face-up card. With two cards placed face-up, the highest exposed poker combination bets first or drops from the game, as above. Thus, an Ace, King outranks a Queen, Jack, and a pair outranks high cards. After the second round of betting, the dealer gives each active player a third face-up card, which is followed by the person with the best exposed hand opening the betting interval. Finally, the dealer gives each active player a fourth face-up card, for a total of five cards, and again the player with the best exposed hand initiates the betting interval, which is followed by the showdown. The player with the best hand wins the pot.

Remedies and Penalties: If the dealer accidently exposes a card before a betting interval is completed, she buries that card and gives the top card to the player who would have received it if the other card had not been exposed. She completes that round of dealing with the person whose card was accidently exposed and buried.

Mexican Stud

Mexican Stud is a variation of Five-Card Stud. The two games differ as follows:
    1. The dealer deals all five cards face down.
    2. On receiving her second, third, fourth, and fifth cards, each player may decide which of her face-down cards to turn face up. Each player must turn a card face up before each round of betting.

Seven-Card Stud

As in Five-Card Stud, the ante is optional. The dealer begins the game by giving the players two cards face down and a third card face up, one at a time, which is followed by a betting interval as described in Five-

Card Stud. The dealer then gives each player her fourth, fifth, and sixth cards face up in three rounds of dealing. After each round of the deal, the players hold a betting interval. Finally, the dealer gives each person her seventh, and last, card face down, which is followed by a final round of betting and the showdown.

In the showdown, each player selects her best five cards as her poker hand. Only in the case of tied hands would the players use their other two cards; in this event, the higher card(s) would break the tie.

Other than the number of cards and betting intervals, Five-and Seven-Card Stud are the same game.

Baseball

Baseball is the same game as Five- and Seven-Card Stud with the following exceptions:

1. All 9s, whether face up or down, and 3s face down ("in the hole") are wild.

2. If a player receives a face-up 3, he must either "buy the pot" (double its value) or drop out of the game. If he buys the pot, thus staying in the game, all 3s are wild whether face up or face down (in the hole).

3. If a player receives a face-up 4, he receives another face-up card immediately as a bonus card. A 4 dealt face down (in the hole) does not earn a bonus card.

As in other Stud games, the player chooses his best five cards as his Poker hand in the showdown.

High-Low Poker

The concept of High-Low can be applied to most Poker games. When applied, the holder of the high hand and the holder of the low hand split the pot. The holder of the high hand always wins the odd chip.

The lowest-ranking hand is called "the runt hand," and it consists of a hand of different suits whose value is less than a pair. Thus, the lowest runt possible is a 2, 3, 4, 5, and 7 of mixed suits. The highest card determines the rank of a runt.

The Showdown Games Group

Black Jack (Twenty-One)

Number of Players and Deck Used: Any number of persons may play this game (four to eight being best) with a 52-card deck and chips. The cards rank as follow: Each Ace counts as either 1 or 11, depending only on the player's need; each King, Queen, Jack, or 10 counts as 10; each 9 through 2 counts as its pip, or index, value.

Chips and Bet: Before the game actually gets under way, the players agree what number of chips constitutes a minimum and maximum wager, or bet. Each player, except the dealer, must place her bet on the table in front of herself before she receives any cards at the beginning of each round of play. The dealer does not need to make a bet, because she is playing against each of the other players for whatever their individual bets may be.

Beginning the Game: In home games, the players draw or cut cards for first deal. High cut wins. The dealer shuffles, and any player may cut. The dealer then *burns* a card, that is, she turns a card from the top of the deck, makes it visible to all players, and turns it face up on the bottom of the deck, if it is not an Ace. If the card is an Ace, the shuffle, cut, and burn procedure is repeated. Some players will allow the dealer to slip the Ace into the deck and to face and burn another card without repeating the entire shuffle, cut, and burn procedure. Then, in rotation from left to right, the dealer gives each player, including herself, one card face down, and then she deals each player, except herself, a second card face down. She deals her second card face up.

The Goal: The goal of the game is the same for all players: to hold cards whose combined pip value is 21 or the nearest possible number below 21 without exceeding 21. (Pips are the markings on the card that indicate the numerical value of the card. A 10, which has 10 pips, has a numerical value of 10.)

"Taking Hits" and Settling Wagers: If the dealer has dealt herself an Ace and any other card with a pip value of 10, she announces "Black Jack" or "Twenty-One" and collects the wagers of the other players. By agreement before the game starts, the dealer may collect double the original bet. If the dealer does not announce Black Jack, each player looks at her face-down cards and mentally calculates their pip value. If any player holds a Black Jack, she announces it and collects double her bet from the dealer.

After the Black Jacks, if any, have been announced and settlements made, each player in turn, beginning with the one at the dealer's left, looks at the dealer's face-up card to help her decide whether she will *stand pat* or *take a hit* and thereby run the risk of going *bust*, or having cards whose count exceeds 21 points. If she is satisfied with her cards, she will say, "I'll stand pat," thereby letting the dealer know that she does not want any more cards. If she is not satisfied with her cards, she will say, "Hit me, " thereby letting the dealer know that she wants one more card. If she wants more than one hit, she will say, "Hit me, again," for each additional card she wants until she is satisfied or goes bust.

Most players will ask for a hit if the pip value of their cards is 16 or less. If the pip value of their cards is 17, most players will stand pat, unless they have cause to believe that the dealer's cards have a larger combined pip value. One such cause might be that the dealer's face-up card is an 8, 9, 10, or Ace. At this point, most players assess the dealer's demeanor and follow their intuition.

If the player asks for a hit and the total pip value of her cards exceeds 21, she admits that fact and forfeits her bet to the dealer. However, if the total pip value of her cards does not exceed 21 and she does not want to chance another hit, she will stand pat. Thus, each player in rotation will decide to stand pat or take a hit.

When the time comes for the dealer to make a decision to stand pat or take a hit, she turns up her hole, or face-down, card to view. The face-up cards of her opponents and her intuition will prompt her to stand pat or take a hit. Most dealers will stand pat on 17, unless their intuition prompts otherwise. (Some players make it a rule that the dealer must stand pat on 17 and collect or pay accordingly.) If the dealer overdraws or exceeds 21, she pays all players who have not overdrawn their bets. If she stands pat, she pays all players their wagers if the pip value of their cards is greater than the pip value of her cards. She does not pay players holding cards with the same or less pip value than the cards she holds. (All ties are won by the dealer.)

In addition to the procedures above for standing pat, taking hits, and setting bets, the following variation of play may occur: If the dealer deals a player two Aces or another pair whose pip value is 10 each, the player may *split the pair*, advance a second bet equal to the first, and play the Aces or other pair as two separate hands. The dealer then deals a card face down to each card of the pair. When a player splits a pair, she must stand pat, take a hit, or otherwise play out the first hand of the pair before playing the second hand.

After the first round of play is completed, the dealer deals the next round from the unused stock. When the entire stock is exhausted, the dealer gathers all discards and repeats the shuffle, cut, and burn procedure given above. The deal customarily passes to a player who has Black Jack when the dealer has not done so at the same time. When this happens, the dealer completes the play for that hand before passing the deck and deal to the new dealer.

Remedies: If it is discovered that the dealer failed to burn a card, she must on demand shuffle the remainder of the deck and do so. A misdealt card can be accepted or rejected by its recipient.

Variations: While the version of Black Jack above is probably the one played most often, there are other versions with slight variations. One such variation is that the dealer gives each player, including herself, one card face down and the second card face up.

A good rule to follow is to make sure that all players understand which version and variations will be in force before starting a game. This is especially important if you are playing in professional gambling casinos like those found in states with legalized gambling.

Spanish Monte

Spanish Monte, a Latin American gambling game, requires a deck of 40 cards (a 52-card deck stripped of its 8s, 9s, and 10s.) Any number of players may participate.

Beginning the Game: The players draw or cut for low card to determine the first dealer-banker. Ace is lowest. After the shuffle and cut, the dealer, holding the deck face down, draws two cards from the bottom of the deck and turns them face up on the table as the bottom layout. Next, he draws two cards from the top of the deck and turns them face up on the table as the top layout. After the dealer forms these two layouts, each player places his bet(s) on one or both layouts.

The Play and Settling Up: After all bets are made, the dealer turns the deck face up to expose the bottom card, which is the *port*, or *gate*, card. If the suit of the port card matches the suit of either card in the top layout, the dealer pays all bets on that layout. The same holds true if the suit of the port card matches the suit of either card in the bottom layout. If the suit of the port card does not match the suits in either the top or bottom layout, the dealer collects all bets made. Thus, the dealer pays for matches in either or both layouts and collects for no matches.

After the dealer and players settle all bets, the former turns the deck face down and gathers up and discards the four layout cards along with the port card. The dealer then forms two new layouts, as above, and again turns the deck face up to expose a new port card. Thus, the game proceeds until the deck is exhausted.

The Euchre Group

The Euchre group of card games has been closely associated with four different countries. In the United States, the game played is Euchre; in Ireland, Spoil Five; in England, Napoleon; and in France, Écarté. Enthusiasts in each country developed their own variations of the game.

The old Spanish game of *Triumphe*, mentioned in an early sixteenth-century manuscript, probably provided the origin of Euchre. The French modified Triumphe and renamed it French Ruff. With the passage of time and more modification, this game became Écarté, which was introduced by the French into the United States in Louisiana.

An interesting observation about these games is that the King outranks the Ace in both Écarté and some versions of Rams *(Ramsch)*, a German descendant of Euchre. In the older games, the King always headed each suit, and the Ace was the lowest card. It was only after political upheaval that the Ace became the highest-ranking card.

Another theory of Euchre's origin is that the game might have resulted from an effort to play the Irish game of Spoil Five with a Piquet deck. The word *Euchre* is of unknown origin, and it means, as does the word Spoil in Spoil Five, to stop or trick the maker of the trump from taking 3 tricks. An interesting note about this theory is that Spoil Five inherited its highest trump card, the trump 5, from the Irish game of Five Fingers, which, in turn, has its origins in an even older Irish card game called Maw, which was popular during the early 17th century. Since the Piquet deck had no 5, it is believed that the players used the second-ranking trump, the Jack, to head the trump suit, which is, of course, characteristic of Euchre.

Euchre

Euchre is a game for four persons (two against two as partners), three persons, or two persons, the last two being played as cutthroat. The game requires a deck of 32 cards (Ace, King, Queen, Jack, 10, 9, 8, 7), or 28 cards (Ace through 8), or 24 cards (Ace through 9). The Joker is sometimes optionally used.

Cards rank as follows: *in trump suit*— the right bower (Jack of trumps), the left bower (Jack of same color), and then trump Ace, King, Queen, 10, 9, 8, and 7; in suit of same color—Ace, King, Queen, 10, 9, 8, 7; *in suits of opposite color*—Ace, King, Queen, Jack, 10, 9, 8, and 7. If the Joker is used, it is the highest-ranking trump, outranking both bowers.

Beginning the Game: In the draw for deal, with Ace being low, low draws play as partners against the high draws. If the Joker is drawn, the player must draw again. After the shuffle and cut, the dealer gives each player five cards (either three and two or two and three), in rotation to the left. The dealer turns the next card face up to propose the trump suit. After each hand, the deal passes to the left.

The dealer must redeal if the deck is imperfect, if there is a card face up in the deck, if she gives the wrong number of cards to any player, if she turns more than one card for trump, or if she does not deal the same number of cards to each player in the same round.

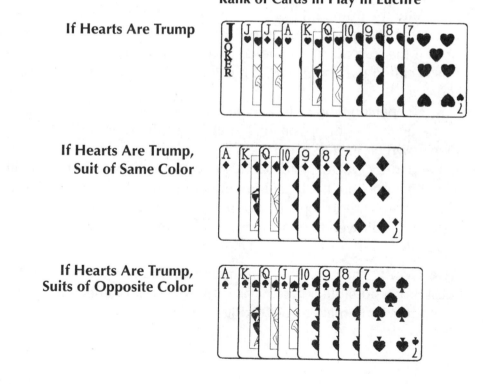

Rank of Cards in Play in Euchre

If Hearts Are Trump

If Hearts Are Trump, Suit of Same Color

If Hearts Are Trump, Suits of Opposite Color

If the Joker is turned for trump, the dealer may, before looking at her hand, declare the suit that the Joker represents to be trump. The players, however, may select such a suit for trump before the game or hand gets under way.

Making the Trump: The player to the dealer's left may say, "I order it up," meaning that she accepts the card turned up and thus proposed as trump by the dealer, or she may pass. If the trump is ordered up, the dealer must immediately discard a card face down from her hand, though she does not take the trump card into her hand before it is her turn to play to the first trick.

If the player to the left of the dealer passes, the dealer's partner may order up the trump by saying, "I assist," or she may pass. If she passes, the next player in rotation has the same option. If all three pass, the dealer may take up the trump or pass. If the dealer passes, she puts face down the card turned as trump. If all four pass, each player in rotation to the left has one chance to name a suit trump, but not the one just rejected, or again pass. The first suit named becomes trump. If all four players pass a second time, the deal is void and passes to the left.

After the trump is taken up, any player may ask the trump maker to name the trump suit, but no one can demand to know its denomination. If the trump is the same color as the face-down proposed trump, this is called *making it next;* if it is the other color, it is called *crossing the suit.*

The person who orders up, takes up, or names the trump may play alone against both opponents. In this case, her partner lays her cards face down on the table and takes no part in the play, but she does share in her partner's victory or defeat. One partner cannot object to the other's going it alone, but the latter must announce her decision to do so when she declares the trump suit. Formerly, a dealer whose partner had assisted was allowed to go it alone; this practice is still observed in some localities.

The Goal: The goal of the trump maker and her partner is to take at least 3 of a possible 5 tricks. The goal of the opponents is to *euchre*, or stop, the trump maker from taking 3 tricks.

The Play: The person to the dealer's left or to the left of the player "going it alone," whatever the case might be, leads any card, and each player in succession plays a card in the same suit, if possible. If not possible, she must either play a trump or discard. It is not necessary to take the trick. If the trick is trumped, the highest trump wins. The winner of each trick leads to the next trick. The winner of each trick must gather it up and quit it, that is, turn it face down. Once quitted, no player may examine the trick until the end of the hand. After 5 tricks have been quitted and tallied for score, the deal passes to the left.

Scoring: If the trump maker and her partner take 3 tricks, they win the hand and the game. If they do not take 3 tricks, they are euchred and they lose the game.

Many Euchre enthusiasts prefer playing a longer game to a score of 5, 7, or 10 points, as agreed to at the beginning of the session. In these games, if the trump maker and her partner take 3 or 4 out of 5 tricks, they score 1 point toward game. If they win all 5 tricks for a *march,* they score 2 points. If the trump maker "goes it alone," she gets 4 points for a march. If the trump maker and her partner fail to get 3 tricks, they are euchred and their opponents score 2 points. Euchre players can use a long-game-scoring procedure with the one-hand, ten-minute game for wagering purposes. In the latter procedure, a scorekeeper keeps a cumulative score until the game ends.

Remedies and Penalties: If a person mistakenly "orders up" or "assists," her side must accept the burden of declaration. If a player names for trump the suit of the rejected proposed trump, her side may not make the trump for that deal.

If a player leads out of turn and everyone plays to the lead, that lead is regarded as valid, and the game continues. However, if the mistake is caught before everyone plays to the erroneous lead, any player may demand that the lead be retracted, left face up on the table, and played at the first legal opportunity. The persons who played to the erroneous lead may restore their cards to their hands without penalty. The opponent who will play last in the next lead of the offending side has the right to name the suit to be led.

133

If a revoke is made but caught before the trick is quitted, the player may substitute a card. However, if the revoke is not caught until after the trick is quitted, or if the offender or her partner accidently or purposely mixes the cards, the players abandon their hands, and the nonoffenders score 2 points. If the revoke is made against a lone hand, the lone player scores 4 points.

Laps

In this variation of Euchre, partners playing the ten-minute game may use any points scored beyond those needed to win a game for wagering purposes. In the 5-, 7-, or 10-point game, each side may carry over to the next game any points scored beyond those needed to win a game.

Slams

Slams is another variation of Euchre. In the ten-minute game, if the trump maker plays a lone hand and takes 5 tricks for a march, she is credited with winning two games. In the 5-, 7-, or 10-minute game, the side that scores 5 points before the opposition can score is credited with winning two games.

Jambone

Jambone, a lone-hand variation, requires the lone hand to lay her cards down face up on the table and to play them. The player to her left my "call up," or name, the first card to be led by the lone player. (Among some Jambone enthusiasts, the players may take turns calling out all the cards from the Jambone hand.) If the Jambone hand wins 5 tricks in the ten-minute game, she is credited with winning two games and scores 8 points for wagering purposes. If not, regular Euchre scoring proceeds.

Jamboree

This variation of Euchre awards 16 points to the maker of the trump if she holds the five highest trumps. She automatically wins the game without having to play a card. The dealer can get credit for a Jamboree by using the turned-up, or proposed, trump card, if needed.

Cutthroat, or Three-Hand Euchre

When three persons play, two persons play in temporary partnership against the maker of the trump. Scoring is the same as in basic Euchre, but if the temporary partners euchre the maker of the trump, they each score 2 points.

Two-Hand Euchre

When two persons play, they strip the 7s and 8s from the deck. All rules applying to the basic four-hand game of Euchre apply to its two-hand variation.

Six-Hand Euchre

When six persons participate, three play against three, and the partners sit alternately around the table. If a lone hand prevails against three opponents, he scores game. Otherwise, scoring remains the same.

Railroad Euchre

Railroad Euchre, a four-hand variation, differs from the basic game of Euchre as follows:

1. The players use the Joker, which ranks above the right bower. They also mutually select a trump suit in advance in case the Joker is turned up as the proposed trump.

2. The player going it alone may, optionally, discard one card and call for her partner's best card. The partner responds and then lays her hand face down on the table during the play. Conversely, if the dealer's partner decides to go it alone, the dealer may give her partner a card from her hand or the turned-up trump, whichever she deems better.

3. Either opponent may also call for her partner's best card to go it alone against the first lone hand. Euchre of a lone hand by two opponents scores 2 points; euchre of one lone hand by another lone hand scores 4 points. Otherwise, the scoring remains the same.

4. Euchre enthusiasts often combine Laps, Slams, Jambone, and/or Jamboree with Railroad Euchre to form variations in the game.

Buck Euchre

Buck Euchre requires four players to use a 24-card deck, plus the Joker; five players, a 28-card deck, plus the Joker; six players, a 32-card deck, plus the Joker. Apart from these basic requirements, Buck Euchre differs from regular Euchre as follows:

1. Each person plays by and for himself in cutthroat fashion.

2. Before the deal, each player puts 1 chip in the pool, as agreed to at the start of the game.

3. The person ordering up or otherwise making the trump must take 3 tricks or put 1 chip in the pool for each trick he fails to take. Each trick taken is worth 1 chip. If a player takes all 5 tricks, he wins the entire pool.

Call-Ace Euchre

The rules governing the number of players, the kind of deck used, and the deal are the same in Call-Ace Euchre as in Buck Euchre. The differences between the two games are as follow:

    1. The Joker is not used.

    2. The dealer turns up the trump, leaving three unknown cards in the four-hand game, two in the five-hand game, and one in the six-hand game.

    3. The player who orders up or names the trump may call out the best card of any suit, except trumps, and the holder of that card becomes her partner. The partner, however, remains unknown until she plays the card called out. Since all cards are not in play, the best card might be a King, Queen, or Jack. It might be that the trump caller is holding that card herslf, in which case she would not have a partner. The trump caller also might say, "Alone," or call on a suit of which she holds the Ace.

    4. If the trump caller and her partner take 3 tricks, they win the hand and the game in a ten-minute game.

If the 5-, 7-, or 10-point game is being played, they each score 1 point; for a march, or 5 tricks, they each score 3 points. If they are euchred, each opponent scores 2 points. A lone hand scores 1 point for 3 tricks. For a march, the lone player scores 1 point for each person playing, including herself, in the game.

SECTION 3
Solitaire Games

A Word About Solitaire Games

What makes the games in this section some of the world's best?

First, every one of them has something about it that is intriguing and challenging—something that makes it especially enjoyable to play.

• You'll find simple counting games that are just right for when you don't want to be overtaxed.

• You'll find complex games that call on every bit of your concentration.

• You'll find games that are irresistible because they have such a great look to them.

• And many are so mesmerizing and compelling that once you start playing them, you can't stop.

Second, all the games are practical. You won't find layouts that you'd have to play on the floor or that require your handling three or four decks of cards.

Third, the ratio between the number of cards you need to lay out and the amount of play in the game is usually a comfortable one. You don't have to lay out two packs of cards only to discover that the game is lost before you even get to make a move! Most of those infuriating games have been eliminated, unless they have a particular fascination of their own—and then you're warned in advance.

All the games in this section are worth trying out—and fun to play. We hope you like them as much as we do, and find a few that become your new favorites.

—Sheila Anne Barry

Before You Begin

We've grouped the one-pack and two-pack solitaire games separately, on the supposition that you probably have only one pack at hand most of the time.

The descriptions at the top of each game will let you know vital information right away—which games are possible to play in a very small area, for example.

They will also tell you which games are easy to win and which are almost impossible—so you know what you're up against.

We've tried to eliminate words that you have to go back and look up, like "reserve" and "tableaux" so you can whip through the instructions and start to play right away.

There are, however, a few terms you need to be familiar with:

Suit—There are four of them: Hearts, Diamonds, Clubs, and Spades.

Suite—A full set of thirteen cards of one suit: Ace to King of Clubs, for example.

To build—To place one card on another to create a sequence—whatever kind is called for. Usually the sequence just goes up or down—the Queen, for example, is placed on the King if the sequence is down, on the Jack if it's up.

Building upward in suit means laying down cards from low to high—from the Ace (or wherever you have to start from)—to the King (or wherever you have to end at)—in one single suit: from the Ace to the King of Hearts, for example.

Building downward in suit means laying down cards from high to low—from the King of Hearts through the ranks to the Ace, for example.

Rank—The card's number. A 10 of Diamonds "ranks" higher than a 9 of Diamonds.

Foundations—The cards that score—the ones you build on. They are usually put up above the layout, as in the most popular solitaire games, *Klondike* and *Canfield*. But sometimes they are place differently—or not placed at all.

The stockpile—The cards that are left in your hand after you have completed the layout.

The wastepile—The collection of discarded cards.

A column—Cards that go vertically in a line.

A row—Cards that go horizontally in a line

Deuces—2s.

Games are arranged alphabetically, but when talking about a prototype game, we've placed the best variations next to it, so that you don't have to leaf back to find the rules for the original game.

Every layout is shown in the book, except when the variations follow a prototype game—or when there's no layout at all, as in *Hit or Miss.*

Solitaire is really the ultimate game—one in which it is very clear that you are competing only against yourself and the run of the cards (sort of like Life?). Win or not, we hope you enjoy playing the games!

One-Pack
GAMES

Accordion

Other Names: Idle Year, Tower of Babel, Methuselah

Space: Small/Moderate.

Level: Difficult.

Play: Start by dealing the cards one at a time face up in a row of four from left to right. Go slowly so that you can keep comparing the cards you deal with their neighbors. Whenever a card matches the card on its left—or third to the left—you move the new card over onto the one it matches. The match may be in suit or rank.

Let's say that the first four cards you turn up are:

The 8 of Spades matches the 8 of Clubs (on its left) and also the 5 of Spades (third to the left). You could move it onto either one. Which one will turn out better? You really can't tell at this point.

Once you move a card over, though, the card on the bottom doesn't have any more significance. The card on top is the one to match.

As soon as you move a card—or a pile—move the later cards over to close up the sequence. That will open up new moves for you, too.

Go on dealing cards, one at a time, stopping after each one to make whatever moves are possible, until you've used up all the cards.

For example, suppose that you deal:

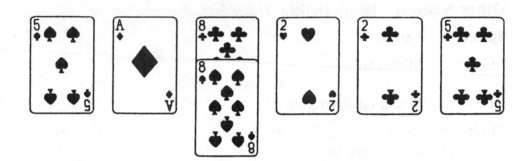

You can move the 2 of Clubs onto the 2 of Hearts. Then close up the row. The 5 of Clubs moves next to the 2s. It's a Club and that's a match! But once you move the 5 over onto the 2 of Clubs, another move opens up: You can move the entire pile over onto the 5 of Spades, which is the third card to the left. So the cards look like this:

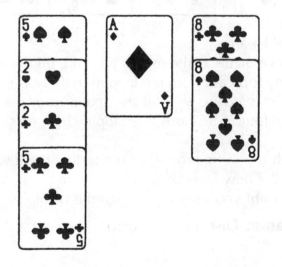

To Win the Game: Get the whole pack into one pile. It's almost impossible. If you end up with five piles, you're doing pretty well.

Aces Up

Other Names: Idiot's Delight, Firing Squad

Space: Smali.

Level: Moderate.

Layout: Deal four cards in a row.

Play: If you have two cards of the same suit, discard the one that is lower in rank. Aces are high.

  For example, here you have:

Discard the 5 of Hearts.

  When you've made all the moves you can, fill the empty space in the row with any top card from the layout. In this case, where there is only one layer of cards as yet, fill the space from the cards in your hand. Then deal four more cards overlapping the one's you've already set up.

  Go through the same process of discarding the lower card of the same suit from the new layer of cards.

  And so on until you've gone through the whole pack.

To Win the Game: Discard all the cards—except the Aces, of course.

Auld Lang Syne

Other Name: Patience

Space: Small.

Level: Very Difficult.

Layout: Deal out all four Aces in a row. Underneath each one, deal a card. These cards are the stock from which you are going to build.

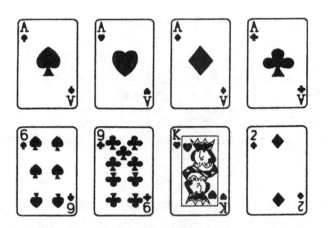

To Win the Game: Build the Aces up to Kings, regardless of suit.

Play: When you've finished the moves you can make with the first set of four cards, deal another row of four right on top of them. Keep going until the stock is exhausted.

Tam O'Shanter

Level: Almost Impossible

Play: Play in exactly the same way as *Auld Lang Syne*, except don't put the Aces up first. Just wait until they show up in the deal.

Baker's Dozen

Space: Wide.

Level: Easy.

Layout: Deal 13 columns of four overlapping cards. Aces will go into a foundation row above the layout.

After you lay out the cards, check on the Kings. If a King is in an exposed position, move it underneath the other cards in the column. If a King is lying on another card of the same suit, place it underneath that card.

To Win the Game: Release Aces and build them up to Kings in suit.

Play: Build downward on the cards in the layout, one card at a time, regardless of color or suit. Do not fill any spaces.

Perseverance

Space: Wide.

Level: Moderate.

Play: Play exactly the same way as *Baker's Dozen*, except:
1. Set Aces in foundation piles from the start.

2. Lay out twelve columns of four overlapping cards each.

3. If a group of cards is in suit and in sequence, starting at the top, you can move the entire sequence as a unit.

4. On the layout, build down in suit only.

5. You have two **redeals**. Gather up the piles in the reverse order of the way you put them down, and then deal them back into twelve columns, as far as they go.

Good Measure

Space: Wide.

Play: Play exactly the same way as *Baker's Dozen*, except:
  1. Deal ten columns of five overlapping cards.
  2. Start with two Aces in the foundation row.

Baroness

Other Names: Thirteen, Five Piles

Space: Moderate.

Level: Easy/Moderate.

Layout: Deal a row of five cards.

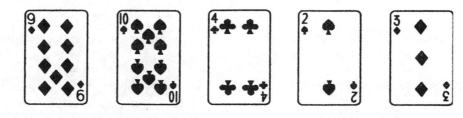

Play: Remove any Kings or any pair of cards that add up to 13. That includes not only:

3 and 10	5 and 8
4 and 9	6 and 7

but also: Ace and Queen and   2 and Jack.

Discard those cards. Then deal the next row of five, on top of the first one, and go through the same process. Only the top cards are available for pairing and discarding.

Deal on, until the pack has been exhausted. The two cards left over at the end can be made into a separate pile. They are also available to be paired and discarded.

To Win the Game: Discard all the cards in pairs that add up to 13.

Redeals: None.

Beleaguered Castle

Other Names: Laying Siege, Sham Battle

Space: Large.

Level: Easy.

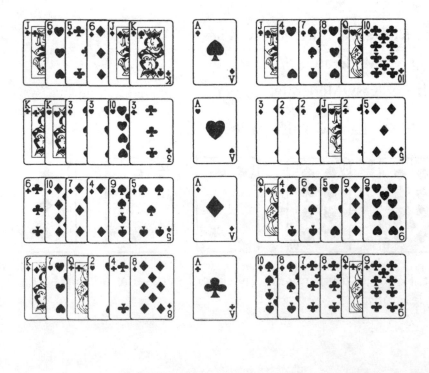

Layout: Lay out the cards in two large wings, each made up of four rows of six overlapping cards. In the middle, place a column of Aces—the foundations.

There is a traditional way to lay out the cards: Start with the Aces in a column in the middle. Then deal out a column of four cards along the left-hand side and a column of four cards at the right-hand side. Then alternate in dealing columns, left and right, until the pack is all laid down.

To Win the Game: Build the Aces up to Kings in suit.

Play: The only cards that may be moved onto the foundations are the completely exposed ones on the ends of the wings. The cards on the ends can also be moved onto each other, regardless of suit, going downward in rank. For instance, in the illustration, the 9 of Hearts could go on the 10 of Spades, but not on the 8 of Diamonds.

Should any row in the wing become empty, you can fill it with any exposed card.

Street and Alleys

Play exactly the same way as *Beleaguered Castle*, except:

1. Do not set up the Aces ahead of time—mix them in with the pack.

2. Deal seven cards to the two top rows of the wings on each side.

Citadel

Play exactly the same way as *Beleaguered Castle*, except:

1. Do not set up the Aces ahead of time—mix them in with the pack.

2. During the process of dealing, you may play any cards to the foundations that they are ready to receive. Once an Ace is in place, for example, you may fill in with deuces, and if deuces are there, you could even build 3s or higher.

When a card is placed on a foundation during the dealing, do not replace it in the layout; just leave its space empty.

3. When dealing, once a card is laid down on the wings, it cannot be moved until the dealing is over.

Betrothal

Other Names: Royal Marriage, Coquette, Matrimony

Space: Large.

Level: Easy.

To Win the Game: Get the Queen of Hearts next to the King of Hearts. And while you try to do this, you eliminate some of the spoilsports who come between other "like" couples.

Layout: Start with the Queen of Hearts at your left. Put the King of Hearts at the bottom of the deck. Deal the cards in a row, one by one, next to the Queen, until the whole pack is out on the table.

Play: While you deal, however, you can throw out certain cards—any one or two cards that get between two cards of the same rank or suit.

For example, in the illustration above, you can remove the 3 of Diamonds and the 5 of Clubs, because they are between two cards of the same rank, the 2s. You can also remove the Ace of Diamonds because it also lies between two cards of the same rank (2s again).

Betsy Ross

Other Names: Musical, Fairest, Quadruple Alliance
Plus Belle, Four Kings

Space: Small.

Level: Moderate.

Layout: Lay out on the table any Ace, 2, 3, and 4. Directly under them lay out any 2, 4, 6, and 8. The four cards on the bottom are foundations. You'll be building on them, but in an odd sort of way.

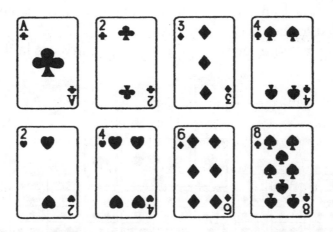

Play: The only purpose of the top row is to remind you of the key numbers you have to build by.

On the 2 you'll build the standard way—by 1s:
2 3 4 5 6 7 8 9 10 J Q K
On the 4 you'll build by 2s:
4 6 8 10 Q A 3 5 7 9 J K
On the 6 you'll build by 3s:
6 9 Q 2 5 8 J A 4 7 10 K
On the 8 you'll build by 4s:
8 Q 3 7 J 2 6 10 A 5 9 K

To Win the Game: Build all the cards into groups of 13 on the foundations.

Redeals: Two.

Bisley

Space: Very wide.

Level: Moderate.

Layout: Remove the Aces from the pack and deal them onto the table as the first four cards in a row of 13. The next nine cards in the pack are then dealt next to them but lower down.

Create three more rows of 13 until all the cards are laid out.

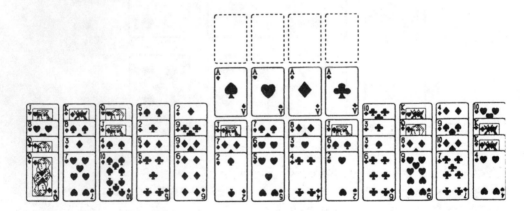

To Win the Game: Build Aces up to Kings in suit and Kings down to Aces.

Play: As they become available, remove the Kings and place them above the Aces. Build on the cards in the layout, upward or downward in suit, playing any cards that you can to the foundations.

Calculation

Other Names: Broken Intervals, The Fairest

Space: Small.

Level: Easy.

Layout: Remove any Ace, 2, 3, and 4 from the pack and set them up in a row. They are your foundations.

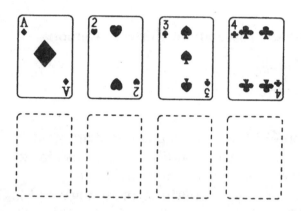

To Win the Game: Build up all the foundations to Kings, each in a different way.

Play: The first card, the Ace, will be built by 1s—the same way you've been building Aces straight along—

 1 2 3 4 5 6 7 8 9 10 J Q K

The second card—the 2—will be built by 2s—
2 4 6 8 10 Q A 3 5 7 9 J K

The third card—the 3—will be built by 3s—
3 6 9 Q 2 5 8 J A 4 7 10 K

The fourth card—the 4—will be built by 4s—
4 8 Q 3 7 J 2 6 10 A 5 9 K

Start by turning over one card at a time, which you can build, regardless of suit, on any foundation that is ready for it. If the card cannot be used on any pile, put it in one of four possible wastepiles underneath the foundations. The top cards of the wastepiles are available to play onto the foundations. The strategy you use to decide where to place an unusable card is crucial. It's okay to keep the cards spread out so you can see what your choices are at any moment.

Canfield

Other Names: Fascination, Thirteen, Demon

Space: Small.

Level: Difficult.

Canfield is one of the most popular solitaire games in the world. A shorter, faster game than *Klondike*, Canfield is played much the same way, but it starts from a different basic layout.

Canfield came by its name in an interesting way. Mr. Canfield owned a gambling house in Saratoga Springs in the 1890s. He used to sell his customers packs of cards at $50 each and then pay them back $5 for every card they were able to score. Estimates are that the average number of cards you could expect to score in a game was five or six, so Mr. Canfield did pretty well.

Layout: Count out 13 cards into one pile and put it in front of you face up and a little to your left. Then put a 14th card to the right of the pile and slightly above it; whatever that card is, it becomes the foundation card of this particular deal. As the other cards of the same rank appear, you'll be placing them too in the foundation row.

To Win the Game: Build the foundation cards into four complete suits of 13 cards each.

Next, you lay out a row of four cards below the foundation card, face up:

No cards are ever built on the 13-pile. The object is to unload it. For example, in the illustration above, you couldn't put a 5—or any other card—on the 6. Cards from the 13-pile can be played only onto the foundations or into the four-card row when a space opens up.

Play: First check the four-card spread carefully to see whether you can make any moves. Besides playing cards to the foundations, you can build cards onto the four-card spread downward in alternating colors.

For instance, in the illustration above, the 3 of Hearts can go onto the 4 of Spades; the 7 of Diamonds can go up into the foundation row; and the 6 of Spades can come down into the row of four. Once it does, the 5 of Hearts can be played onto it.

You are permitted to move sequences of cards as one unit. For example, the 3 and 4 may be moved together onto the 5 and 6, so your layout would look like this:

Then you can proceed to fill the other open spaces in the four-card row with cards from the 13-pile.

Now start turning up cards from the pack, in batches of three, playing them either to the foundations, to the four-card row or to the wastepile. The top card of the wastepile is always available for play.

As spaces open up in the four-card row, continue to fill them with cards from the 13-card pile. When these are exhausted, you can fill them with cards from your hand or from the wastepile.

Redeal: As many times as you want, or until the game is blocked.

Selective Canfield

Play exactly the same way as *Canfield*, except deal a five-card row instead of four. Choose your foundation yourself from one of these cards.

Rainbow

Play exactly the same way as *Canfield*, except go through the pack one card at a time. You are allowed two **redeals** in some versions of the game—none in others!

Storehouse

Other Names: Provisions, Thirteen Up, Reserve

Space: Small.

Level: Easy.

Play: Play exactly the same way as *Canfield*, except:
    1. Remove the four deuces from the pack and set them up as the foundations.
    2. Build them up in suit to Aces.

Superior Demon

Level: Moderate.

Play: Play exactly the same way as *Canfield*, except:
    1. Spread the 13-card pile so that you can see it and take it into account as you play.
    2. You don't have to fill a space in the layout until you want.
    3. You can shift any part of a sequence to another position—you don't have to move the entire sequence.

Chameleon

Play in exactly the same way as *Canfield*, except:
1. Count out only 12 cards instead of 13 for the 13-card pile.
2. Deal only three cards to the four-card row.
3 The layout looks slightly different, like this:

The Clock

Other Names: **Hidden Cards, Four of a Kind, Travellers**
                   Sundial, All Fours, Hunt

Space: **Moderate.**

Level: **Difficult.**

Layout: Deal the pack into 13 face-down piles of four cards each. Arrange 12 of them in a circle, representing the numbers on a clock dial. Put the 13th pile in the middle of the circle.

It should look like this:

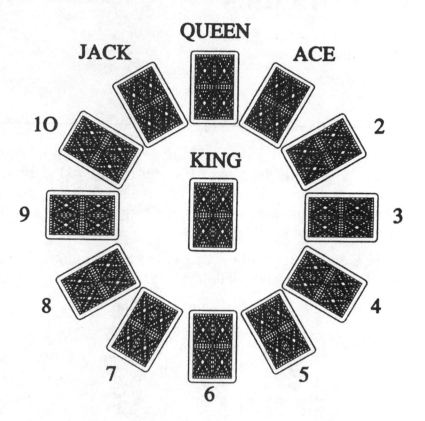

Play: Start by picking up the top card of the middle pile. Suppose it's a 5. Slip it, face up, under the pile of cards that are in the 5 o'clock position. Then pick up the top card of the 5 o'clock pile. Suppose it's a Jack. It would go under the 11 o'clock pile (remember, the King pile is in the middle of the clock—and the Queen is at 12). And you would pick up the top card of the 11 o'clock pile and slip it under whatever pile it belongs in.

When you slip the fourth card of any group into place—and there is no face-down card to turn over—turn over the top card of the next highest card pile.

To Win the Game: Get all the cards turned face up before the fourth King is turned face up.

Double or Quits

Space: Small.

Level: Easy.

Tricky building—and on only one foundation!

Layout: Deal seven cards in a sort of frame shape, as shown below. Then place a card inside the frame. That card is the foundation, and you can build on it from the frame or from the stockpile. If any of the cards in the layout turn out to be Kings, put them on the bottom of the deck and replace them with other cards.

To Win the Game: Build all the cards onto the foundation—except for Kings—doubling the value of the card that has just been placed.

Play: For example, let's say the layout looks like this:

The card you've got to build on is a deuce, so you deal out the cards, one by one, until you come to a 4 of any suit—and place that on the deuce. The cards that you go through before you come to the 4 go on the wastepile.

The next card you need to find is double 4—or an 8. There is one in the frame, so you can use that right away. Spaces in the frame are filled with the top card of the wastepile or, if there is no wastepile, from your hand.

Double 8 is 16. So deduct 13 (the number of cards in a suit) and you get 3: This is the card you need to find next.

So—a sequence goes like this:

2 4 8 3 6 Queen (12) Jack (11) 9 5 10 7 Ace 2

and the sequence repeats.

Redeals: Two

Duchess

Other Name: Glenwood

Space: Small.

Level: Moderate.

Layout: Lay out four fans of three cards each at the top of the table. Leave a space for the foundations, and then deal out a row of four cards.

To Win the Game: Build the four foundation cards into full 13-card suites.

Play: Choose any one of the exposed cards in the fans to be your foundation. For example, in the illustration above, it might make sense to choose the 3 of Diamonds as your foundation, because the 3 of Spades is available to build onto the foundation and so is the 4 of Diamonds.

After you make all possible moves to the foundations, you can start building downward on the row of cards, in alternating colors. You are allowed to move all the cards of one pile onto another pile as a unit, when the cards are in the correct sequence (down by suit).

Go through the stockpile of cards, one by one, building to the foundations or the layout or discarding the unplayable cards to the wastepile.

When spaces open up in the row, fill them from the fans—and when no fans are left, from the wastepile.

Redeals: One.

Eagle Wing

Other Names: Thirteen Down, Wings

Space: Moderate.

Level: Difficult.

Layout: Deal 13 cards and place them face down in a pile in the middle of the table. This pile is known as "the trunk." Then lay out four cards, face up, on one side of the pile, and four cards face up on the other. These are the "wings" of the eagle.

Deal out one more card and place it directly above the pile, so that your layout looks like this:

That last card is a foundation pile. As other 8s appear, they go up in a row alongside it and you build on them as well.

To Win the Game: Build the foundations up to full 13-card suites.

Play: Go through the cards, one by one. If you cannot play a card onto one of the foundation piles, put it in a wastepile. The top of the wastepile is always available for play.

You can also build with the cards in the wings. When a space opens up in the wings, fill it right away with a card from the trunk. The bottom card in the trunk—if you get that far—may be played directly to the foundation without waiting for a place in the wings.

In the building, Aces follow Kings.

Redeals: You are allowed two (three times through the cards).

Fortress

Other Name: Fort

Space: Large.

Level: Difficult.

Layout: Deal out five columns of five cards each on both sides of the playing space. Lay out the entire deck, face up, adding an extra card to the top rows.

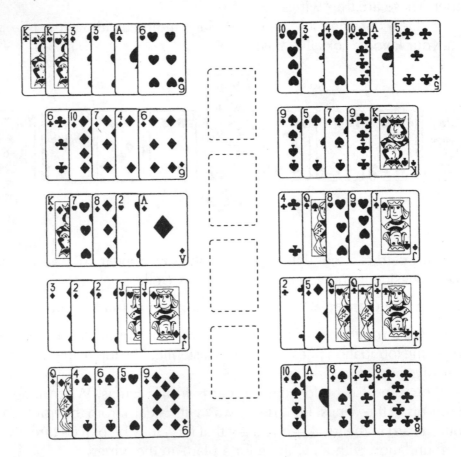

Foundations—Aces, as they become available—are placed in the middle column, as in the illustration.

To Win the Game: Build up the Aces in suit to Kings.

Play: After playing whatever cards you can to the foundations, you can start building in suit on the exposed cards in the layout, one card at a time. You can build up or down on the layout, but not both ways in the same row.

Chessboard

Other Name: Fives

Play: Play in exactly the same way as *Fortress*, except instead of putting Aces in the foundation column, choose whatever card you want after dealing out the layout.

Fourteens

Other Names: Fourteen Puzzle, Fourteen Out, Take Fourteen

Space: Large.

Level: Easy.

Layout: Deal the cards, face up, in 12 columns of four cards each. You'll have four cards left over. Just put them on the first four columns. Arrange the cards so that you can see them all.

Play: Remove pairs of available cards whose totals add up to 14. There will be, of course:

Ace and King	4 and 10
2 and Queen	5 and 9
3 and Jack	6 and 8

Available cards are the ones that are exposed at the bottoms of the columns.

To Win the Game: You win when all the cards have been discarded.

Gaps

Other Name: Spaces

Space: Large.

Level: Difficult.

Layout: Deal all the cards in the pack—in four rows of 13 cards, each face up.

Then remove the Aces. This leaves gaps in the layout. These gaps must be filled by the card that is next higher in rank to the card on the left— and in the same suit. For example, suppose the gap opens up to the right of a 3 of Hearts. It must be filled by a 4 of Hearts.

If the gap opens up in the first space at the left of a row, it may be filled with any deuce.

If the gap opens up after a King, it cannot be filled. Action is blocked. When a King blocks the action in every row, the deal is over.

To Win the Game: Get each row into a sequence of cards from 2 to King, by suit.

Redeals: As many as you want. You need to gather up the cards in a special way for the redeal. Leave in place the deuces that appear at the left end of a row and any cards that follow it in the correct sequence and suit. For example:

Leave these   but not these

Then, gather up all the not-in-place cards, shuffle them, and deal them out as follows:

    1. Leave one gap to the right of each sequence.
    2. If the only card in place is a 2, leave a gap to the right of it.
    3. If there is no 2 in the row, leave a gap at the start of the row, so that a 2 can be moved in.

The Garden

Other Names: Flower Garden, Parterre, Bouquet

Space: Large.

Level: Easy.

Layout: Deal out six columns of six overlapping cards. This is "the garden."

Spread the remaining cards out in front of you. They are "the bouquet." The layout looks like this:

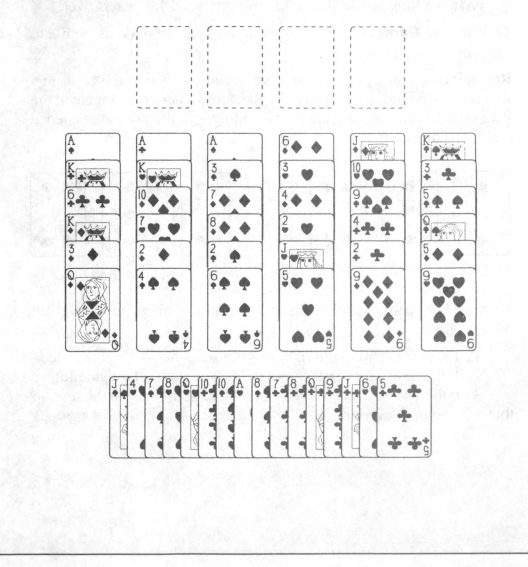

The cards spread out at the bottom are available to play onto the layout, building down one by one regardless of suit.

As the foundations—the Aces—become available, they are placed above the layout.

To Win the Game: Build the Aces up in suit to Kings.

Play: Start building on the exposed cards at the bottom of the columns, one card at a time, and to the foundations. If a complete column is cleared away, the space may be filled by any available card. Every card of the bouquet is available for building at all times.

Golf

Space: Moderate.

Level: Difficult.

Layout: Deal seven rows of five cards each, so that the layout looks like this:

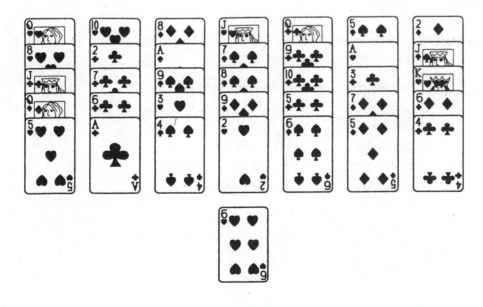

Deal one card below that will start the wastepile.

To Win the Game: Get rid of the entire layout by building up and down on the wastepile, regardless of suit.

Play: Only the exposed cards of the layout are available for building. In the example above, the 5 of Hearts can go on the wastepile; the 4 of Spades can go on that, opening the way for the 3 of Hearts. Then you can go in the other direction with the 4 of Clubs, and so on.

You can't build anything on a King. When you put a King on the wastepile, you've ended the sequence. Whenever you end a sequence—by putting down a King or not being able to make another move—you can take a card from the stockpile of 17 cards that never got into the layout. Place the card on the wastepile and resume play. If you use up all the cards in the deck, and still have cards in the layout, you've lost the game.

Grandfather's Clock

Space: Huge.

Level: Easy.

Layout: Remove the following cards from the deck and place them in a circle, as in the following illustration:

2 of Hearts	8 of Diamonds
3 of Spades	9 of Clubs
4 of Diamonds	10 of Hearts
5 of Clubs	Jack of Spades
6 of Hearts	Queen of Diamonds
7 of Spades	King of Clubs

These are the foundations on which you are going to be building a "real" clock face.

Place the remaining cards in eight columns of five cards each. Overlap the cards so you can see them all.

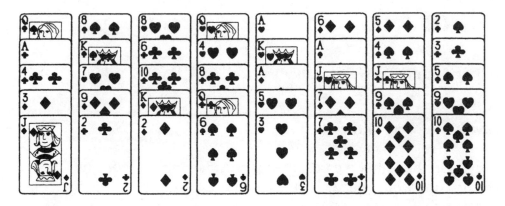

Play: Using the exposed cards in the layout, build the foundations—the cards on the clock face—up in suit until the cards on the top correspond to the numbers on a real clock face (with Jack as 11 o'clock and the Queen at 12).

In order to free the cards to do this, build on the cards in the layout—downward, regardless of suit.

Spaces may be filled by any available card.

To Win the Game: Get the clock to have the right number values on its face, as in the illustration below:

Hit or Miss

Other Names: Treize, Talkative, Roll Call, Harvest

Space: Small.

Level: Very Difficult.

Play: Go through the cards one by one, naming each one as you go. The first one would be "Ace," the second "Deuce," the eleventh "Jack," and so on.

When your name and the rank of the card are the same, it's a *hit*, and you get to discard the card.

You are allowed to go through the cards as many times as you want—or until you go through the entire pack twice without a hit.

To Win the Game: Discard every card in the deck.

King Albert

Other Name: Idiot's Delight

Space: Large.

Level: Easy.

Layout: Deal a row of nine cards face up. Then deal a row of eight cards face up on top of them, leaving the first card uncovered. Continue placing rows of cards, each one card less than the row before, leaving the first card uncovered.

    You'll have seven cards left when you finish laying out the cards. These are "free" cards, which you can use any way you want—on the layout or the foundations.

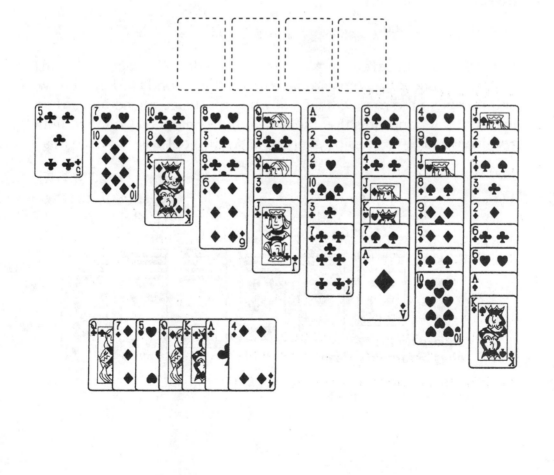

To Win the Game: Release the Aces and build them up to Kings in suit.

Play: Once the cards are laid out, play whatever you can to the foundations, which you set up above the layout. Then build on the layout itself—downward in alternating colors.

Only one card at a time may be built on the foundations or the layout.

A space may be filled by any available card.

Klondike

Other Names: Canfield, Fascination, Triangle, Small Triangle, Demon Patience

Space: Moderate.

Level: Difficult.

Layout: Lay out seven cards in a row—face down except for the first card. Then put the eighth card face up on the second card in the row, and complete the row with face-down cards. Place a face-up card on the third pile, and finish off the row in the same way. Continue until you have a face-up card on every pile. Your layout will look like this:

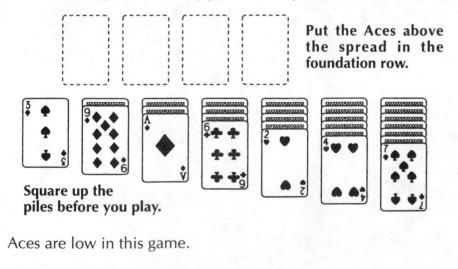

Put the Aces above the spread in the foundation row.

Square up the piles before you play.

Aces are low in this game.

To Win the Game: Build up complete suites from Ace to King.

Play: First, look over the spread carefully. Move any cards that you can to the foundation row—Aces and any cards you can build on them.

You can also build cards on the layout itself. Only the face-up cards are available for this building, and only if they are the exposed cards of the pile. Then you can build downward in alternating colors.

In the example, shown here, you can move the Ace to the foundation row, and then move the black 3 onto the red 4, and the red 2 onto the black 3.

Every time you move a face-up card, you need to turn up the face-down card beneath it. When there are no more face-down cards in a pile, you have a space. Spaces can be filled by any available King.

When you've made all the moves you can, start going through the stockpile one by one, looking for more cards to build onto the foundations and the layout. If you can't place the card, it goes face up onto a wastepile, and the top card of the wastepile is available for play.

Scoring: Five rounds make a game. Add up the number of foundation cards you've come up with in each round for your final score.

Klondike by Threes

This game is exactly the same as *Klondike,* but you go through the stockpile of cards by threes. Because of that, you get redeals. Rules vary about how many redeals you get. Some say two (three trips through the cards), and some say as many as you want.

Redeals: Two (or more).

Agnes

Space: Moderate.

Level: Moderate.

Play: Play exactly the same way as *Klondike*, except:

1. When you finish the layout, deal the next card above it to make the first foundation. Aces, of course, need to be played between the Kings and 2s.

2. Below the layout, deal a row of seven cards. These are available to be played onto the layout and the foundations. Play as many of them as you like, and when you have no more moves to make, deal another seven cards on top of them. You'll probably have spaces in that row of seven; be sure not to skip them when you deal the second row. After you deal a third layer of seven cards, you'll have two cards left in your hand. Turn them face up. They are available too.

3. Spaces in the layout may be filled by any card that is one lower than the foundation card. For example, if the foundation card is a 2, the spaces can be filled only with Aces.

Whitehead

Level: Moderate/Difficult.

Play: Play exactly the same way as *Klondike*, except:

1. Deal all the cards face up.

2. Instead of building in alternate colors, build red on red, black on black.

3. When spaces open up in the layout, fill them with any available card or group of cards.

4. When moving piles of cards as a unit, you may do it only where the cards are in sequence by suit.

Thumb and Pouch

Level: Easy

Play: Play exactly the same way as *Klondike*, except:
1. When building, a card can be laid on any card that is one rank higher regardless of color—except one of its own suit.
2. A space may be filled by any available card or sequence of cards.

La Belle Lucie

Other Names: The Fan, Clover Leaf, Alexander the Great
Midnight Oil, Three Shuffles and a Draw, Fair Lucy

Space: Large.

Level: Moderate.

This is one of the most delightful solitaire games.

Layout: Lay out the whole deck in sets of three, face up.

One single card will be left over, which becomes a set of its own.
    The only cards that may be moved are the exposed ones on top of the sets. They are built up on the foundations or on the top cards of other sets, by suit, building downward.

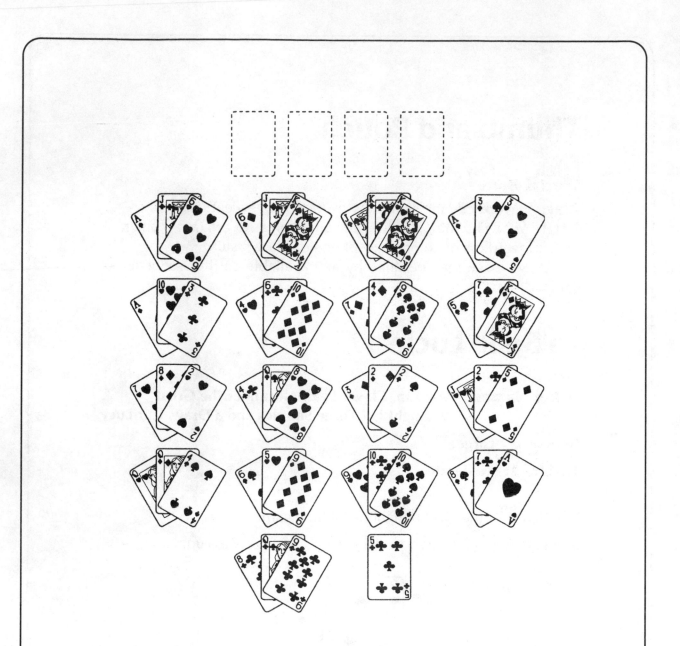

To Win the Game: Release the Aces and build them up in suit to Kings.

Play: Once you have the cards laid out, move the Aces that are available onto the foundations. In the example above, the Ace of Hearts is available for one of the foundations; so are the 2 and 3 of Hearts. Then proceed to build on the top cards of the fans, one card at a time. When a fan is entirely eliminated, it is not replaced.

Redeals: Two. To redeal, gather up the fans, shuffle the cards, and set down in groups of three as before. Any leftover cards are sets by themselves.

Special Bonus: In the last redeal, when you're stuck, you get one free move—one card you can pull from underneath one or two others and play in any way you want.

Super Flower Garden

Level: Easy.

Play: Play exactly the same way as *La Belle Lucie*, except building takes place regardless of suit.

Trefoil

Other Name: Les Fleurons

Play: Play exactly the same way as *La Belle Lucie*, except you put the Aces in a foundation row before laying out the fans. You'll then have 16 complete fans.

Shamrocks

Other Name: Three-Card Fan

Level: Easy.

Play: Play exactly the same way as *La Belle Lucie*, except:
    1. If a King is on the top of a set and a card of lower rank in the same suit lies under it, you can put the King under that card.
    2. No fan may contain more than three cards.

Little Spider

Space: Small.

Level: Moderate.

Layout: Lay out four cards face up in a row along the top of your playing space, and four cards in a row beneath them—leaving space for a row in between. That's where the foundations will go—two Aces of one color and two Kings of another—as they become available:

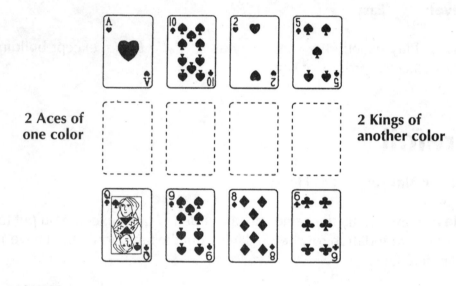

2 Aces of one color

2 Kings of another color

To Win the Game: Build the Aces in suit to Kings and the Kings in suit to Aces.

During the Deal: You can move any card from the top row onto the foundations. But you cannot move a card from the bottom row unless it can be moved straight up into place—into the position directly above its original position. For example, in the illustration on the left on page 183, the 2 of Hearts can go on the Ace of Hearts, but in the illustration on the right, it can't.

Play: When you've made all the moves you can to the foundations, deal another four cards to the top and bottom rows. Make your moves, and then deal again—until all the cards have been laid out.

At this point, the special rules that for "During the deal" no longer apply. You can move any card from the top or bottom rows onto the foundation piles. You can also build top cards from the layout onto each other regardless of suit or color—up or down.

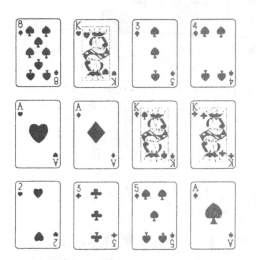

2 of Hearts can go straight up onto the Ace, because the Ace is the same suit.

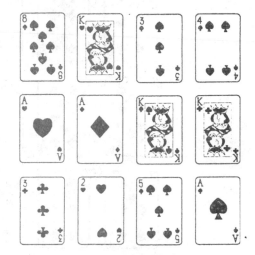

2 of Hearts cannot go onto the Ace, because it is not directly under the Ace of Hearts.

Spaces in the layout may not be filled. Kings may be placed on Aces.

Monte Carlo

Other Name: Weddings

Space: Moderate.

Level: Moderate.

Layout: Deal five rows of five cards each, so your layout looks like the illustration on the next page.

To Win the Game: Discard the entire deck in pairs of the same rank. You can discard them if they are:

1. Next to each other
2. Above or below each other
3. "Touching" diagonally

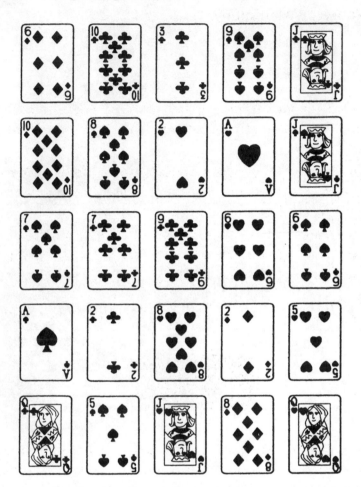

Play: Remove every pair that you can from the layout. When you do, there will be holes. Close up the cards so that all the holes are filled and the cards are in the same order in which you laid them out.

After you make the cards into solid rows again, deal new cards to make up the bottom rows, so that you have five rows of five cards again.

Remove the pairs again in the same way, and when you can't move any more cards, go through the process of closing up the spaces in the layout and filling in at the end with cards from your hand.

Nestor

Other Name: Matrimony

Space: Moderate.

Level: Moderate.

Layout: Deal eight cards face up in a row. Then deal another five rows overlapping them, so that you can see all the rows at one time.

As you deal, make sure you don't have any cards of the same rank in a column. If you're about to deal a deuce onto a column where a deuce already appears, slip the card underneath the pack and deal another card instead.

You'll have four cards left over when you finish dealing. They are the stock.

Play: Remove cards of the same rank by twos from the exposed cards at the ends of the columns. When you can't make any more moves, turn up the first card of the stockpile. If that won't help you, turn up the next, and the next.

To Win the Game: Discard the whole layout by twos.

Osmosis

Other Name: Treasure Trove

Space: Small.

Level: Moderaste.

Layout: Deal four sets of four cards each face down. Then square them off face up and put them in a column at the left side of your playing space. Place the next card in the deck (which becomes the first foundation) to the right of the top card.

Place additional foundation cards (other cards of the same rank), as they become available, in a column under the first.

To Win the Game: Build each foundation card to a full 13 cards in suit but regardless of sequence.

Special Building Rule: No card may be placed in the second, third, or fourth foundation rows unless a card of the same rank has already been placed on the previous foundation card.

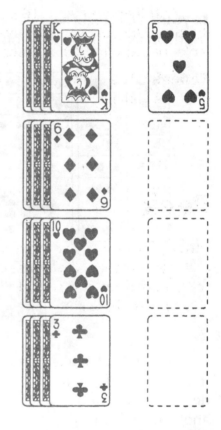

Play: Let's see how this works. In the illustration the foundation card is the 5 of Hearts. The first thing to do is to build any other Hearts that are already showing on the table—such as the 10 and the King—and put them alongside the 5, overlapping, so you can see what cards have been played to this foundation.

Then start going through the cards in the stockpile, three at a time, to find additional Hearts and more foundation cards for the other suits.

Let's say you turn up a 5 of Clubs. You place it below the 5 of Hearts.

The next card you turn up is a Queen of Clubs. You cannot place it—because the only cards that have been placed in the Hearts row are the King and the 10. So those are the only Clubs you could put down beside the 5 of Clubs.

The next card you get is the 5 of Diamonds, and you place it under the 5 of Clubs.

And then you get a 10 of Diamonds. You cannot place it next to the 5 of Diamonds—even though there is a 10 of Hearts out on the table, because the 10 of Clubs has not yet been placed.

Redeals: You get to go through the cards until you win the game—or until the game is blocked.

Peek

Play: Play exactly the same way as *Osmosis*, except with the face-down cards turned up and spread so that you can see them all.

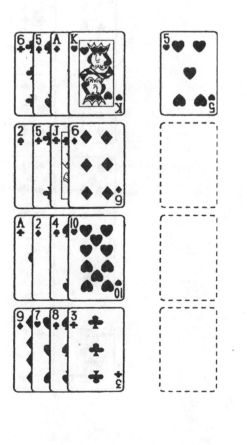

Poker Solitaire

Other Name: Poker Squares

Space: Moderate.

Level: Moderate.

Layout: Deal 25 cards in five rows of five cards each. Each row and each column is a poker hand; so, in any game, you have ten hands with which to build your total score.

To Win the Game: Come up with the highest score.

Play: Rearrange the cards in the layout so that you have the highest-scoring poker hand possible. In some versions of this game, after you move a card once, you cannot move it again.

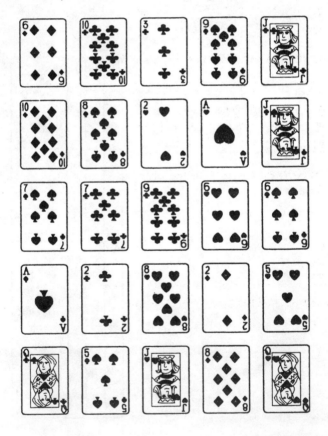

SCORING	American	English
Royal Flush: Five of the same suit in sequence starting with an Ace	100	30
Straight Flush: In sequence, five of the same suit	75	30
Four of a Kind: Four of the same rank	50	16
Full House: Three of a kind plus two of a kind	25	10
Flush: Five of the same suit, but not in sequence	20	5

Straight: Five in sequence, but not in the same suit	15	12
Three of a Kind	10	6
Two Pairs	5	3
One Pair	2	1

Pyramid

Other Name: Pile of 28

Space: Moderate.

Level: Difficult.

A sad thing about many solitaire games is that you play a round—or five rounds—and then it's over. You have no special feeling of victory (unless you've played out and won) and no standard with which to compare your score.

Here's a game that keeps you counting and scoring all the time. You can play it against yourself, against another player, or against "par."

Layout: Lay out the cards in the shape of a pyramid, starting with one card at the top and placing two cards that overlap it, then three overlapping them, and so on, until you have a large triangle with seven cards at its base. Each card has its own numerical value (face value); Kings count as 13, Queens as 12, and Jacks as 11.

Play: Your job is to remove pairs of cards that add up to 13, with this catch: You cannot remove a card unless it is "exposed"—not covered by any other card.

For example, in the pyramid above, you can remove the 7 and the 6 from the bottom row. This opens up the Ace in the row above, which you can remove with the Queen (worth 12) in the bottom row.

You can remove Kings alone, because they add up to 13 without any help.

Place all the cards you remove in a special "Removed" pile, face up. The top card in this pile can be used again to form another 13-match.

Now you start dealing out the rest of the pack, one by one. If the card you turn up does not form a match with an available card in the pyramid, put it into a wastepile. Don't mix up this pile with your "Removed" pile.

If one of the cards you turn up from your hand is a match with the top card of the "Removed" pile, you can remove both of them.

To Win the Game: You need to remove the entire pyramid plus the cards in your hand.

Redeals: Two.

HOW TO SCORE PYRAMID

A match is six games. Score each game as follows:

50 points—If you get rid of your pyramid in the first deal (once through all the cards in the deck).

50 points minus—If you get rid of the pyramid during the first deal but still have cards in your hand or in the wastepile, score 50 points minus the number of cards in the wastepile.

35 points minus—If you get rid of the pyramid during the second deal, but still have cards in your hand or in the wastepile, score 35 points minus the number of cards in your hand and the wastepile.

20 points minus—If you get rid of the pyramid during the third deal, score 20 points minus the number of cards in your hand or the wastepile.

0 points minus—If you never do succeed in getting rid of your pyramid, deduct one point for each card left in the pyramid as well as each card left in your hand and the wastepile. That's right—a minus score!

"Par" is 0 for six matches. If you do better, you've won!

Quadrille

Other Names: Captive Queens, La Française, Partners

Space: Moderate.

Level: Easy.

Layout: The layout for this game is set up as you play. The design that is to be created appears below:

Play: Start turning up cards from the deck. As soon as the 5s and 6s appear, put them in place and start building on them.

On the 5s you build down: **4 3 2 Ace King.**

On the 6s you build up: **7 8 9 10 Jack.**

The Queens just sit in the middle and look regal.

To Win the Game: Build the 6s up in suit to the Jacks and the 5s down in suit to the Kings.

Redeals: Two.

Queen's Audience

Other Name: King's Audience

Space: Moderate.

Level: Easy.

Layout: Make a square of four cards to a side, like this:

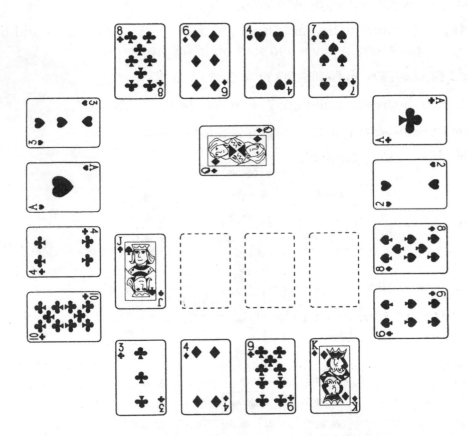

This is the Queen's antechamber. The space inside it is the Queen's Audience. Into the Audience will go the Jacks, as they appear. They are the foundations.

To Win the Game: Build the foundations from Jack to deuce in suit.

Special Buiding Rule: Before a Jack can get into the Queen's Audience, an Ace of the same suit has to go with him. That Ace can come from the walls of the antechamber or from the stockpile. Put the Ace under the Jack.

Kings and Queens get to come into the Audience also, but only in pairs of the same suit. Put the King under the Queen.

Play: Go through the cards one by one, building to the foundations and discarding Queen and King sets into the Audience.

Spaces in the antechamber wall should be filled right away from the top card of the wastepile or the stockpile.

Russian Solitaire

Space: Large.

Level: Very Difficult.

Some people say this is the most difficult solitaire game in the world to win. In any case, it is one of the most intriguing.

Layout: Lay out the cards exactly as you lay them out for *Klondike*, but when you finish, deal the rest of the pack face up on top of the layout, as in the illustration on page 196.

To Win the Game: Free the Aces from the layout and build them up to Kings in suit in a row above the layout.

Play: First, move any Aces that are exposed onto the foundations. Then build downward in suit on the exposed cards of the layout. In order to do this, you will often have to move more than one card at a time—sometimes as many as a whole column of unrelated cards.

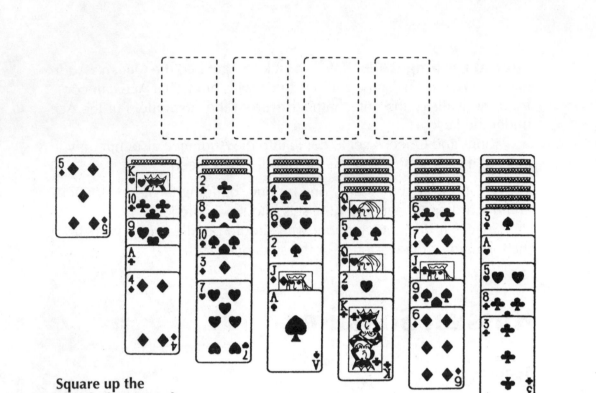

**Square up the
piles before you play.**

In the illustration above, for example:

First, you would move the Ace up to the foundation row, just as in *Klondike*. Then, you would start looking at the other cards that are exposed. The 6 of Diamonds is lying open. You could put the 5 of Diamonds on it, thereby creating a space in the layout. That vacant spot, just as in *Klondike*, can be filled with any King. Suppose you decided to move the King of Hearts. You would have to move the entire column of cards on top of the King to the #1 space. There is only one card underneath the King. Turn it over: it's the King of Diamonds. And it is now the leading card of the second column.

Your next move might be to put the 4 of Diamonds on the 5 of Diamonds. That would open up the Ace of Clubs, which you can put up at the top in the foundation row.

You might then move the 6 of Hearts down onto the 7. Remember that when you move the 6, all the cards on top of it must move too.

Now your layout would look pretty crazy, like the illustration on the next page.

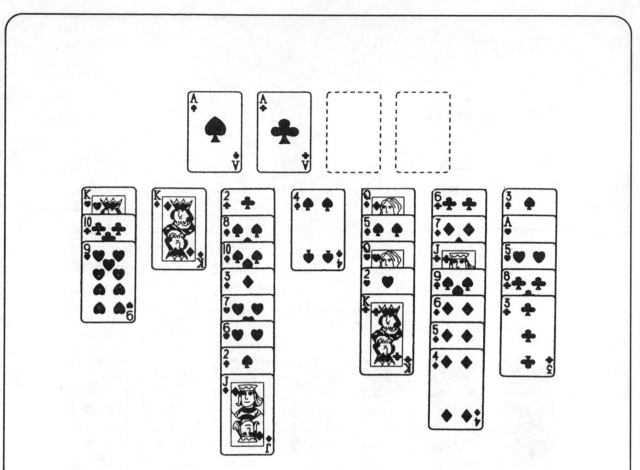

Well, you get the idea.

Play five rounds of this game, adding up the number of points in each for your total score.

Yukon

Level: Moderate.

Play: Play in exactly the same way as *Russian Solitaire*, except building on the bottom cards of the layout is done regardless of suit in alternating colors.

Scorpion

Space: Large.

Level: Moderate.

Layout: Deal a row of seven cards—four face down and three face up. Repeat this same pattern in a second and third row, overlapping the cards each time. Then deal out all the rest of the cards face up on top of this beginning setup. You'll have three cards left over at the end. Put them aside for a few minutes. Your layout will look like this:

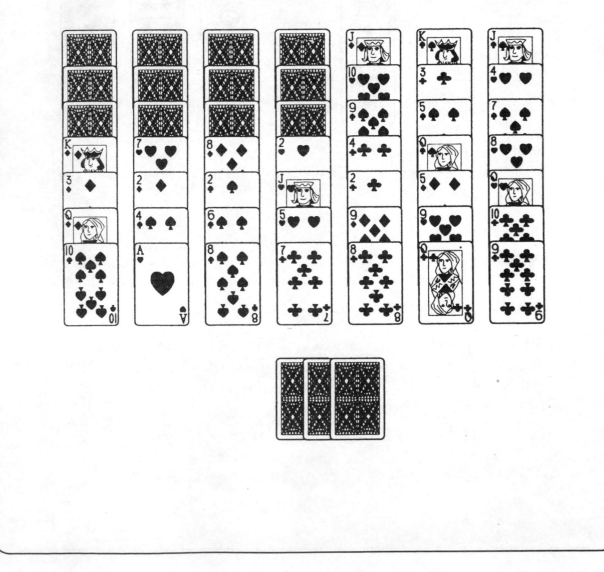

Play: Now you are going to build downward in suit on the exposed cards of the layout. You are not limited to moving one card at a time. You may move any card that meets the requirements of rank and suit— even if it is covered with cards. You just move all the cards with it.

As columns are emptied, you can fill them with Kings—along with the cards that are on top of them. Nothing can be built on an Ace.

When you have exhausted all chances for moves, take the three cards you set aside at the start and place one on each of the bottom cards of the left-hand columns. That picks up the game and can give you a few new moves.

To Win the Game: Build four Kings, right on the layout, with their full suits, like this:

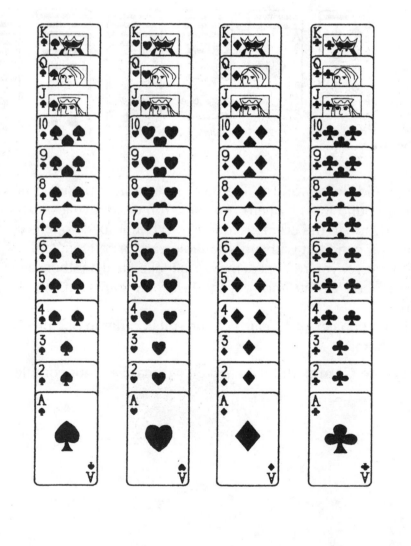

Spiderette

Space: Moderate.

Level: Difficult.

When you're tired and angry at playing *Klondike* and never playing out, you might want to get even with this Cheater's version.

Layout: Lay out the cards the same way you would for *Klondike*, but this time, you're not going to set up any foundation piles.

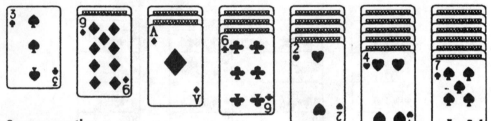

Square up the piles before you play.

Play: Build downward on the layout, regardless of suits and colors (but try to build in suit where you can). You can move groups of cards when they are in the correct sequence. When a space opens up in the layout, you can fill it with any available card or sequence of cards.

    Whenever you run out of moves to make, deal another seven cards on the layout. At the end, put the last three cards on the first three columns.

    When you get all 13 cards of one suit in order in one pile, you can discard them.

To Win the Game: Build up and then discard all four complete suits.

Vanishing Cross

Other Names: Corner Card, Corners, Four Seasons, Czarina

Space: Small.

Level: Moderate.

Layout: Place five cards on the table in the shape of a cross. This is the layout. Then place another card in the upper left-hand corner. That is the foundation. The other foundations—the same rank as the corner card—should be placed in the other corners as they become available.

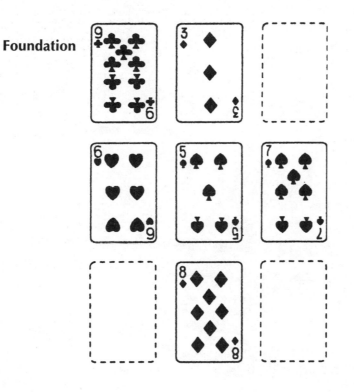

Play: Build whatever cards you can onto the foundation, upward in suit. Then build whatever cards you can onto others in the cross—downward and regardless of suit. When you've exhausted all the possibilites, start going through the stockpile, one card at a time, playing it to the foundation (going up), to the cards in the cross (going down), or, if unplayable, to a wastepile.

To Win the Game: Build all the corner cards into four suites.

Note: Aces may be placed on Kings.

Two-Pack
GAMES

British Square

Space: Moderate.

Level: Easy.

Layout: Deal four rows of four cards each, face up. Four Aces, one of each suit, as they become available, will be placed above the layout as foundations.

To Win the Game: Build the Aces up to Kings in suit—and here's the tricky part—then place another King of the same suit on top of that King and build down in suit to Aces.

Play: Besides building on the foundations, you also build on the layout, up or down in suit. You can build in either direction, but once you decide on a particular direction for any given pile, you have to keep it that way for the entire game.

When you've made all the moves you can make in the layout and to the foundations, start turning over one card at a time to play to the foundations, the layout, or to a wastepile.

You may fill spaces from the top card of the wastepile or from your hand.

Busy Aces

Space: Small.

Level: Easy.

Layout: Deal two rows of six cards each, face up. Aces, as they become available, are foundations and are placed in a row above.

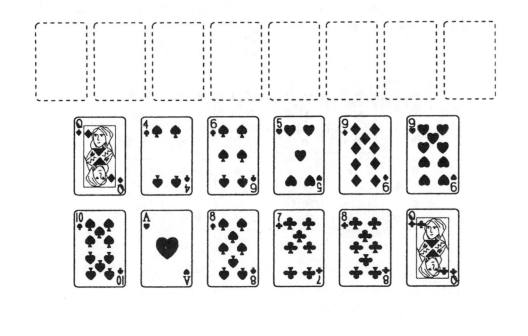

Play: Do whatever building you can at the start on the foundations. Then, build on the layout, downward and in suit. After you've made all the moves you can, begin turning over cards one by one, discarding unplayable cards onto a wastepile.

When spaces open up in the layout, fill them from your hand or the wastepile.

To Win the Game: Build all eight Aces up in suit to Kings.

Capricieuse

Space: Moderate.

Level: Easy.

Layout: Select one Ace and one King of each suit, and place them in a single line.

Then deal out the rest of the pack in 12 face-up piles.

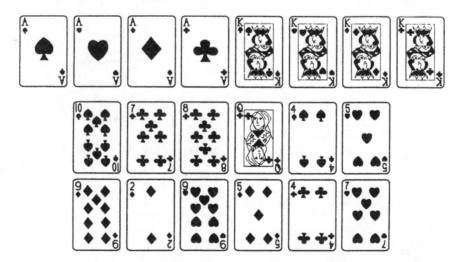

Play: As you deal the cards onto the piles, play any appropriate card from your hand onto the foundations. *Only* cards from your hand can go onto the foundations during the deal—be sure not to move any from the layout.

Don't leave any blanks in the layout as you deal—give a card to each pile. If one card can be played onto the foundation, substitute another card for it in the layout.

When all the cards have been dealt, start building them on each other, in suit.

Kings may not be put on Aces, nor Aces on Kings.

Redeals: Two. When gathering up the cards for a redeal, pick them up in reverse sequence from the way you dealt them.

Congress

Other Name: President's Cabinet

Space: Small.

Level: Difficult.

Layout: Deal a column of four cards to the left and a column of four to the right. Leave enough space between them for the foundations, eight Aces.

To Win the Game: Build the Aces upward in suit to Kings.

Play: First, make whatever moves you can to the foundations. Then, start turning over the cards in your hand one by one, building downward on the layout, regardless of suit, and playing whatever cards you can to the foundations. Fill in spaces from the wastepile or from your hand. Any card on top of a pile is available for building.

Cotillion

Other Name: Contradance

Space: Small.

Level: Moderate.

Layout: Select one 5 of every suit and one 6 of every suit. These are the foundations. Set them up like this:

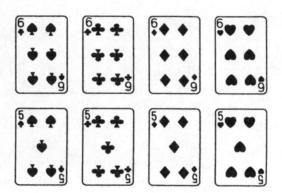

Play: Go through the balance of the cards one by one and play them to the foundations in suit wherever you can.

To Win the Game: Build the 6s up to Queens and the 5s down (through Aces) to Kings.

Redeals: One.

Crescent

Space: Large.

Level: Moderate.

To Win the Game: Build Aces up to Kings in suit and Kings down to Aces in suit

208

Layout: Select one Ace and one King from each suit and place them in two rows, Kings on top.

Then deal the rest of the cards in a semicircle around them in 16 piles. Put the first five cards face down, the top card face up.

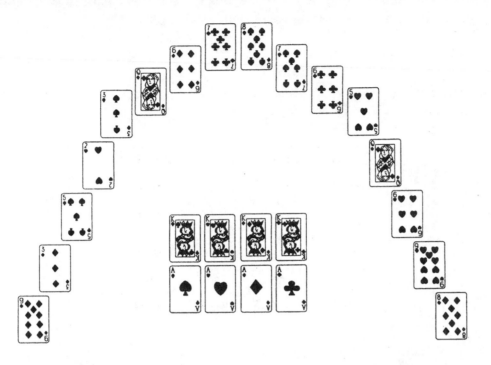

Play: Play whatever cards you can to the foundations. Then you can start building up or down on the layout in suit. When you move the top card of a pile, turn up the card underneath.

When you use up all the cards in a pile and you have an empty space, it cannot be refilled.

Shifting: When you can't make any more moves, take the bottom card from each pile and place it on top of the pile, face up. You need to do this with every pile before you stop to make any moves. You can make this unusual shifting move three times during the game; it's a little like having three redeals.

Reverse: When the top cards of two foundations of the same suit are in sequence, you can transfer one or more cards from one foundation to the other. The original Ace and King may not be transferred.

Open Crescent

Play exactly the same as *Crescent*, but lay out the cards face up and spread them so that you can see them as you play.

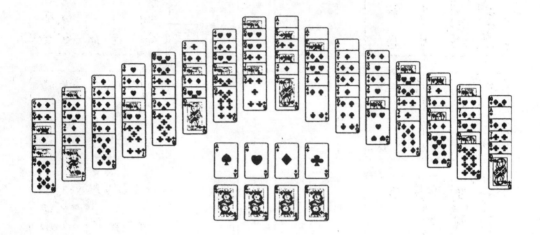

It's a more interesting game when strategy comes into play.

Diplomat

Space: Moderate.

Level: Easy.

Similar to the one-pack *Streets and Alleys*, this game is fairly quick to set up and has lots of action.

Layout: Deal four columns of four overlapping cards, leaving space between them for two columns of side-by-side Aces, which are the foundations as they become available.

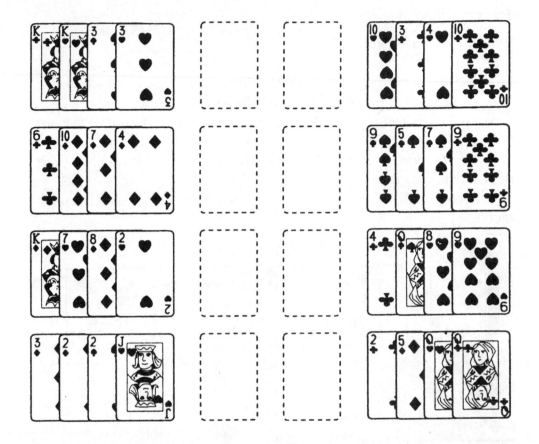

To Win the Game: Build the Aces up in suit to Kings.

Play: After making whatever moves you can to the foundations, you build downward on the exposed cards of the layout, regardless of suit.

When you can't make any more moves, start turning over the cards in your hand, one by one, playing what you can to the layout. Place the unused cards in a wastepile. The top card of the wastepile, the card in your hand, and the exposed cards in the layout are all available to play onto foundations, onto the layout, and to fill any spaces that open up in the layout.

Redeals: One. Just turn over the wastepile.

The Fan

Space: Wide.

Level: Easy/Moderate.

Layout: First, count out 12 cards in one unit. This is the stockpile. Place it face up at the left. Beside it, place an overlapping string of 12 face-up cards. The next card in your hand will be a foundation card. Let's say it's the 10 of Clubs. Leave space next to it for placing the other 10s—seven more of them, as they become available. They will be foundation cards on which you build up from 10s through Aces to 9s.

Underneath this foundation row, deal out four cards from the pack, face up.

To Win the Game: All foundations are to be built in sequence, regardless of suits, until they contain 13 cards. But whether you build upward or downward is up to you. You can make up your mind after you see how the game is shaping up. You don't have to decide until you're ready to start building, but whatever you decide, it will apply to all the foundations.

Play: Start playing onto the foundations by going through the cards in your hand—one by one. Unplayable cards go into a wastepile.

You can also play onto the foundations with the following cards:
1. the top card of the stockpile
2. the exposed card on the end of the string of overlapping cards
3. the four-card row
4. The top card of the wastepile

If a space opens up in the row of four cards, fill it from the wastepile or the cards in your hand.

Redeals: You get two redeals (that means going through the cards three times).

Forty Thieves

Other Names: Big Forty, Napoleon at St. Helena, Cadran
Roosevelt at San Juan

Space: Large.

Level: Moderate.

Layout: Deal four rows of ten cards each, overlapping, as in the picture. Aces, as thet become available, are moved up above the layout as foundations.

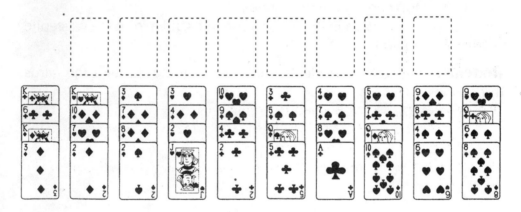

To Win the Game: Build all eight Aces to Kings in suit.

Play: First, build what you can to the foundations. Then build on the layout itself, downward in suit. For example, in the illustration above, the 2 of Diamonds can be placed on the 3 of Diamonds. The Ace of Clubs can be played up to the foundation row. So can the 2. When you have exhausted all the possibilities, start going through the cards one by one, building onto foundations or layout or discarding the unplayable cards into a wastepile. The top card of that wastepile is available too.

When a space opens up in the layout, you can fill it with any card—one from the layout, the top card from the wastepile, or a card from your hand.

Streets

Space: Large.

Level: Moderate.

Play: Exactly the same as *Forty Thieves*, except build downward on the layout in alternating colors.

Indian

Space: Large.

Level: Easy.

Play: Exactly the same as *Forty Thieves*, except:

   1. For the layout, deal 30 cards in three rows of ten cards each. The first row should be face down.

   2. When building on the layout, cards may go on any suit *except* their own.

Rank and File

Other Names: Dress Parade, Deauville, Emperor

Space: Large.

Level: Moderate.

Play: Exactly the same as *Forty Thieves*, except:

   1. For the layout, deal the first three rows face down.

   2. Build downward on the layout in alternating colors.

   3. When all the cards on the top of a pile are in correct sequence, you're allowed to move them as a unit onto another pile in the layout.

Lucas

Space: Large.

Level: Easy.

Play: Exactly the same as *Forty Thieves*, except:
    1. Set up the Aces in the foundation row before dealing the layout.
    2. For the layout, deal three rows of 13 cards each. This makes for a much easier game.

Maria

Space: Large.

Level: Moderate.

Play: Exactly the same as *Forty Thieves*, except:
    1. For the layout, deal four rows of nine cards each.
    2. Build downward on the layout in alternating colors.

Number Ten

Space: Large.

Level: Moderate.

Play: Exactly the same as *Forty Thieves*, except:
    1. Place the first two rows face down.
    2. Build downward on the layout in alternating colors.
    3. When all the cards on the top of a pile are in correct sequence, you're allowed to move them as a unit onto another pile in the layout.

Frog

Other Names: Toad, Toad-in-the-Hole

Space: Moderate.

Level: Easy/ Moderate.

Layout: Count out 13 cards and place them in one pile face up. Make sure no Aces are within the pile. If there are any, replace them with other cards.

    Then place one Ace next to the pack as a foundation. As other Aces appear, they should be placed next to it.

To Win the Game: Build all the Aces up by suit to Kings.

Play: Go through the stockpile, card by card. When cards are unplayable, place them in a row of their own underneath the foundation row—a row of five piles. You can put the cards in any position you choose—all in one pile, if you want.

Fanny

Level: Moderate.

Play: Exactly the same as *Frog*, except:
1. Count out only 12 cards instead of 13 for the face-up pile.
2. Do not set up an Ace to start the foundation row.

Grand Duchess

Other Name: Duchess of Luynes

Space: Small.

Level: Moderate.

Layout: Deal four cards in a row face up and an additional two cards face down to the side. Above them you'll be placing two rows of foundations, Aces (one of each suit) and Kings (one of each suit), as they become available.

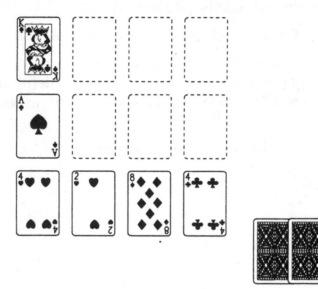

To Win the Game: Build the Aces up in suit to Kings and the Kings down in suit to Aces.

Play: Make any possible moves and then deal again—four cards on top of the cards you dealt before and two more cards face down to the side. Make your moves and continue in this fashion, until you've gone through the entire pack.

　　Then turn up the face-down cards, spreading them out and playing any cards you can to the foundations and making whatever moves are possible.

Redeals: Three (four times through the cards). When you get ready to redeal, pick up the piles in reverse order so that the pile at the right is on the top. Put the face-down pile at the bottom.

    The first two redeals are done just as before, spreading out the face-down pile at the end. The last one is different; don't deal any cards face down to the side. Just deal the four cards onto the layout. Don't build up a face-down pile at all.

Parisienne

Play exactly the same as *Grand Duchess*, except lay out the Aces and Kings at the start.

The Harp

Other Name: **Klondike (with two packs of cards)**

Space: **Large.**

Level: **Easy.**

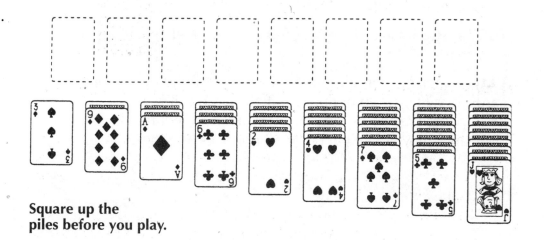

Square up the piles before you play.

Play: Exactly the same as *Klondike*, except:

    1. Use two packs of cards.

    2 Use a nine-card row instead of a seven-card row.

    3. There is no limit to the number of times you can go through the cards, one by one. Do it until you win or until the game is obviously blocked.

    4. When filling a space, you may use an available King, as in *Klondike*, or you may use a group of cards in correct sequence that has a King at the top.

House in the Wood

Other Name: Double Fan

Space: Large.

Level: Easy.

This is a two-pack version of *La Belle Lucie*. But it works out much more often.

Layout: Lay out 34 fans of three cards each, plus one fan of two cards. The top cards of each fan are available for building onto foundations or onto other top cards.

To Win the Game: Free Aces from the fans and build them up in suit to Kings.

Play: After making all initial moves, start building on the exposed cards in the fans—up or down, but always in suit.

    Spaces created by clearing away a fan are not filled.

    Kings may not be put on Aces, nor Aces on Kings.

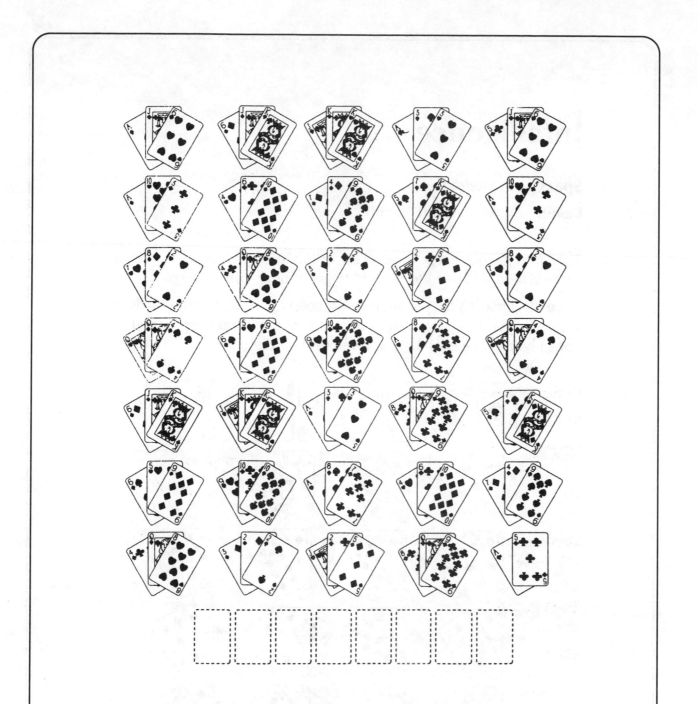

House on the Hill

Play exactly the same as *House in the Wood*, except instead of eight Aces as foundations, lay out one Ace and one King of each suit. Build the Aces up in suit to Kings and the Kings down to Aces.

Intelligence

Space: **Moderate.**

Level: **Moderate/Difficult.**

Similar to the one-pack *La Belle Lucie*, but tougher, this is an intriguing game where you need to be bold to get enough cards into play.

Layout: Deal 18 fans of three cards, keeping the rest of the cards in a stockpile. As you deal, if Aces appear, put them right on the foundations and replace each one with the next card.

To Win the Game: Build the eight Aces up in suit to Kings.

Play: Once you've moved all the cards you can to the foundations, you can start building on the exposed cards of the fan, as you would in *La Belle Lucie*, up or down, in suit. You may reverse direction on the same pile.

Each time you completely eliminate a fan, you may replace it with three new cards from your hand. That is the only way to get new cards into play.

Kings may not be put on Aces, nor Aces on Kings.

Redeals: Two. While redealing, you still have the chance to pull Aces out of the fans, replacing them with the next card from your hand.

Matrimony

Space: Moderate.

Level: Difficult.

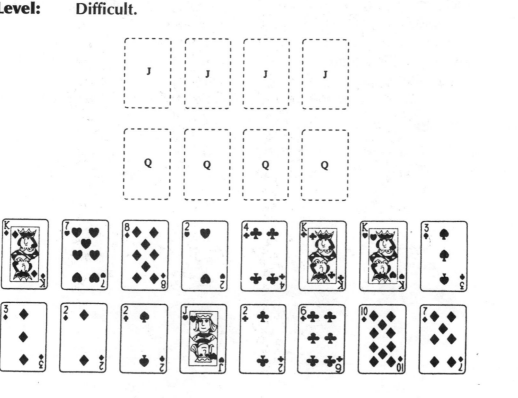

Layout: Lay out two rows of eight cards each. Then, as they become available, place four Queens of each suit and four Jacks of each suit above these rows, as foundations.

To Win the Game: Build the Queens upward in suit through Aces to Jacks, and the Jacks downward in suit through Aces to 10s.

Play: First, move any cards you can from the layout onto the foundations. Then deal 16 cards onto the layout—one on each card—or space (spaces are not filled except by this 16-card deal).

Make whatever moves you can and then, when you get stuck, deal another 16 cards onto the layout. The last deal will be only six cards, but deal it in the same way.

After you have used up all the cards in the deck and made all possible moves, pick up the pile in the lower right-hand corner, turn it face down, and deal the top card face up on its own place. Then continue dealing the pile, on each card in turn, starting at the upper left-hand corner.

Make any moves you can as a result of this play. Then, when you're stuck, pick up the 15th pile, turn it over, and deal that pile, first putting the top card in its own place and going on from there.

Again, make what moves you can. When you're stuck, pick up the next pile to the left and continue the process, until you've gone through all the piles once.

If you get stuck after dealing out pile number one, you've lost the game.

Miss Milligan

Space: Moderate.

Level: Difficult.

To many, this is the ultimate solitaire game.

Layout: Deal out a row of eight cards. Move all Aces up above the row of cards, as they become available. The Aces are foundations.

To Win the Game: Build all eight Aces upward in suit to Kings.

Play: Besides building on the foundations, you also can build within the original row of eight cards—downward in alternating colors.

When you've made all possible moves, deal out another eight cards that overlap the original eight, filling in spaces as you go.

Play off what you can to the foundations, build what you can on the row, and deal another eight cards onto the layout.

Continue this process until you've used up all the cards in your hand. At this point you have the object of "weaving."

Weaving: This is the option of removing one card from the bottom row of the layout temporarily—while you make other moves. When you get that card back into play—either on a foundation or the layout—you are then allowed to remove another card. You can keep doing this until you win the game or you can't find a place for the card.

Special Rules: You are permitted to move two or more cards as a unit—when they are built correctly in rank and sequence and at the end of a column. For example, in the diagram below, you can move the 10 of Diamonds, 9 of Spades, and 8 of Hearts as a unit onto the Jack of Clubs.

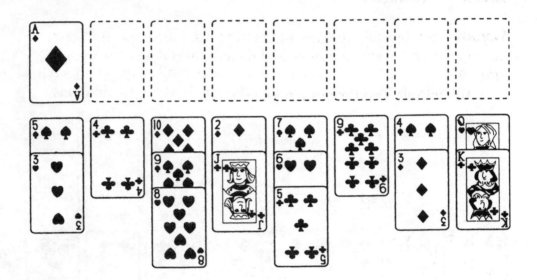

Spaces may be filled with any available King or with a sequence that leads off with a King.

Mount Olympus

Space: Large/Moderate (for alternate layout).

Level: Easy.

Layout: Remove all the Aces and deuces from the pack and set them out in an arch, alternating Aces and deuces, and colors, as in the picture.

All the Aces and deuces are foundations.

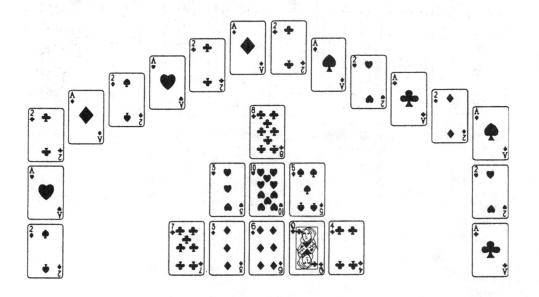

Then place nine cards in a pyramid shape beneath the arch.

To Win the Game: Build the foundations upward in suit by 2s: from Aces to Kings, deuces to Queens.

The Aces build like this: **A 3 5 7 9 J K**

The deuces build like this: **2 4 6 8 10 Q**

Play: You may also build on the cards in the pyramid in the same way—skipping a card as you go. Build them downward in suits.

When cards are in the correct rank and sequence, you can shift an entire pile as a unit.

When a space opens up in the pyramid, fill it at once with a card from the stockpile.

When you have made all possible moves and filled the spaces, deal nine more cards onto the pyramid. Make whatever plays you can onto the foundations, and then deal another nine cards. Continue this process until the stockpile is gone.

Note: If you don't have enough space to create the layout shown on page 227, you can set out the cards like this:

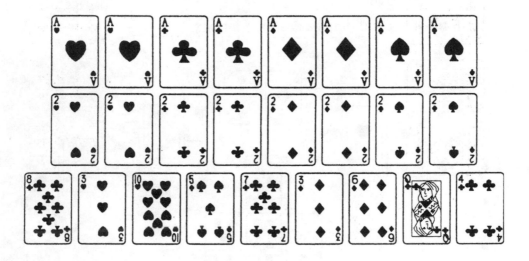

It is also an easier game to play in this format, because it is easier to build on the layout.

Napoleon's Square

Other Name: Quadruple Line

Space: Moderate.

Level: Easy.

To Win the Game: Build all the Aces upward in suit to Kings.

Layout: Deal 12 piles of four cards each, four piles to the left (place them horizontally), four to the right (horizontally), and four across the top of the layout. All eight Aces will be placed in two rows in the middle of the layout as they become available.

Play: First, make all the moves you can. Move Aces to the foundations and then build on the layout itself, downward and in suit. The top card of any pile is available and so are groups of cards that are in sequence and in the same suit.

When a space opens up in the layout, fill it with any available card or group of cards in sequence and the same suit, or from your hand or from the wastepile.

After all initial moves have been made, turn over one card at a time from your hand, discarding unplayable cards to the wastepile. The top card of the wastepile is always available for play.

Odd and Even

Space: Moderate.

Level: Moderate.

Layout: Deal three rows of three cards each. These cards are available for building on foundations.

Play: Start going through the cards in your hand one by one. As soon as an Ace comes up, start a foundation row above the layout. As soon as a two comes up, place it in that row also, as shown in the picture.

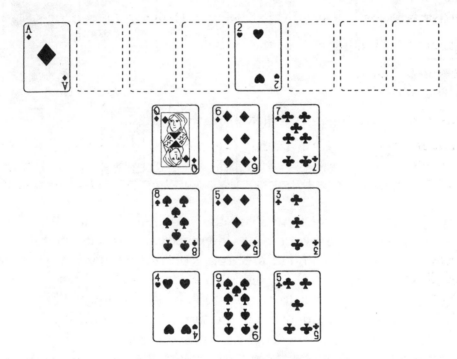

Eventually, you need to place three more Aces and three more deuces in the foundation row. One of each suit should be represented.

   If you can't play the card from your hand onto the foundations, put it in a wastepile.

   If a space opens up in the group of nine cards, fill it right away from the wastepile, or—if there is none—from your hand.

To Win the Game: Build the foundations upward in suit to full 13-card sequences—but you need to do it by 2s!

The Aces should build like this:

A 3 5 7 9 J K 2 4 6 8 10 Q

The deuces should build like this:

2 4 6 8 10 Q A 3 5 7 9 J K

Redeals: One.

Panama Canal

Other Names: Precedence, Panama, Order of Precedence

Space: Moderate.

Level: Easy.

This is almost as simple as a game can get.

Layout: The layout starts with only one card in place—a King. That card will be followed by seven additional cards—the Queen, Jack, 10, 9, 8, 7, and 6 of any suit—as they become available. These are foundations.

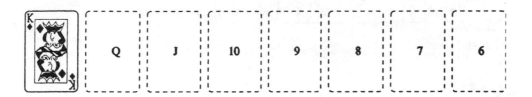

To Win the Game: You need to build each foundation downward and regardless of suit into a sequence of 13 cards.

Play: Start going through the pack, one card at a time. The catch is that you have to place the Queen before you can put down the Jack, and the Jack must be in place before you can place the 10, and so on, down to the 6. You are free, though, to build on the cards that are already in place. For example, you can put a Queen on the King that is already on the table and a Jack on the Queen. Unplayable cards go into a wastepile whose top card is always available.

Circular Sequence: Kings may be built on Aces when the foundation card is something other than an Ace or King.

Redeals: Two.

Queen of Italy

Other Names: Terrace, Signora

Space: Moderate.

Level: Easy.

Layout: Deal 11 cards at the top, overlapping each other, face up. Then deal three cards face up: you get the opportunity to choose from these three which one will be your foundation. You make this choice based on the 11 cards you've already laid out.

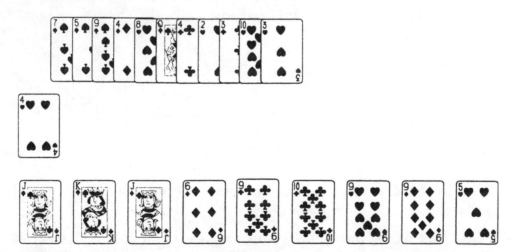

After you decide on a foundation card, put it in place below and to the left of the first row. Then, use the two cards you did not select for the foundation to start a nine-card row at the bottom. Deal another seven cards from the stock. This nine-card row is where the action takes place. You may play the cards to the foundations as they become available. You can also build them on each other downward in alternating colors. Only one card at a time may be moved from the layout.

To Win the Game: Build your foundation cards into eight complete 13-card sequences in alternating colors.

Circular Sequence: Kings can be built on Aces, if your foundation card is something other than an Ace or King.

What about those 11 cards at the top? They are out of bounds, playable only onto the foundations, as they become exposed.

Play: Start by making what plays you can to the foundations and within the layout. When you can't make any more moves, go through the cards in your hand one at a time. Play what you can to the foundations and the nine-card row. Put unplayable cards in a wastepile. The top card of the wastepile is always available for play.

Spaces in the nine-card row may be filled from the top card of the wastepile or from the stockpile. Never add any cards to the 11-card overlapping row.

Falling Star

Play exactly the same as *Queen of Italy*, except:
1. The overlapping row represents stars that have to fall for the game to be won.
2. The next card (the 12th) becomes the foundation.

Blondes and Brunettes

Other Name: Wood

Play exactly the same as *Queen of Italy*, except:
1. Deal only ten cards in the overlapping row instead of 11.
2. Skip the three-card choice of foundation. The next card becomes the foundation card.
3. Deal nine cards for the bottom row.

General Patience

Other Name: Thirteen

Play exactly the same as *Queen of Italy*, except:
1. Deal 13 cards instead of 11 for the overlapping row at the top.
2. Build in suit rather than in alternating colors.
3. You do not actually get a redeal, but you are allowed to turn the wastepile over and play until you reach an unusable card. Then the game is over.

Royal Cotillion

Space: Large.

Level: Moderate.

There's something especially intriguing about this game, which is not surprising, considering that it is one of the most popular of the two-pack games.

Layout: First, to your left, deal out three rows of four cards each. To your right, deal out four rows of four cards each. Leave a space between them that is wide enough for two cards which will be the foundation columns. As they become available, move one Ace and one deuce of each suit into this center section.

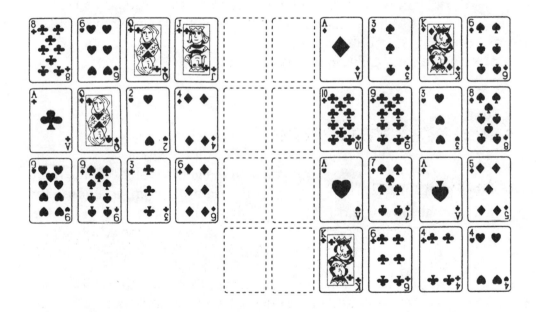

To Win the Game: Build the Aces and deuces in the middle section upward by suit to a full 13-card sequence. The building must be by twos, as follows.

Aces should build:

A 3 5 7 9 J K 2 4 6 8 10 Q

Deuces should build:

2 4 6 8 10 Q A 3 5 7 9 J K

Play: Go through the cards one by one, building onto the foundations if you can or to the wastepile if you can't.

The cards that are off to your right can all be played onto the foundations, and as soon as spaces open up in this group, you can fill them from the wastepile—or if there is no wastepile, from your hand.

The cards that are off to the left, however, have only one active row—the bottom one. You can't move the cards in the second row until the bottom ones have been moved away. For example, in the illustration, only the 9 of Hearts, the 9 of Spades, the 3 of Clubs, and the 6 of Diamonds would be available to play onto the foundations. Spaces in the left-hand group are never filled in.

Gavotte

Other Names: Odd and Even

Space: Large.

Level: Easy.

Play: Play exactly the same as *Royal Cotillion*, except:
1. Lay out four rows of four cards on the left as well as on the right.
2. Either the left-hand group or the right-hand group can be the one that moves and is filled in. Take your choice, but whichever way you decide, you need to keep it that way for the whole game.
3. Foundations can be whatever cards you choose—3 and 7, Queen and Jack—whatever.

236

Royal Rendezvous

Other Names: None

Space: Moderate.

Level: Easy.

There's enough variety in this game to make it fun, even if there are few surprises!

Layout: First, lay out all eight Aces in two rows, one on top of the other. Each row should have one Ace of each suit. Then lay out one deuce of each suit—two on each side of the bottom row, as in the picture. Underneath this row, deal out two rows of eight cards each. They can be played onto the foundations.

To Win the Game: Build up all eight Aces and four deuces in suit as follows:

1. The top row of Aces gets built up in suit to Queens.
2. The bottom row of Aces gets built up by twos to Kings, like this:

   A 3 5 7 9 J K
3. The deuces get built up by twos to Queens, like this:

   2 4 6 8 10 Q
4. Four Kings get put at the top of the layout—but not until after their counterparts have already appeared in the lowest foundation row.

Play: Go through the cards, one by one, and build them onto the foundations if you can. If not, discard them to a wastepile. If a space opens up in the bottom two rows, you must fill it with the top card of the wastepile, or, if there isn't any, with the card from your hand.

St. Helena

Other Names: Napoleon's Favorite, Washington's Favorite, Privileged Four

Space: Moderate.

Level: Easy/Moderate.

With its odd and changing rules, this game has a peculiar fascination. Maybe that's why Napoleon is said to have played it while in exile. Others say that's unlikely because the game hadn't even been invented then. There's an enormous amount of laying out of cards, but in the end, it's worth it.

Layout: Start by removing one Ace and one King of each suit from the cards and setting them up in 2 rows, Kings on top. These are your foundations.

Then deal out the rest of the pack in 12 piles clockwise: four on top, two on the right side, four on the bottom of the foundations, and two on the left side, as in the illustration.

Keep on dealing, one card on each of the 12 piles, until you've laid out all the cards.

To Win the Game: Build the Aces up in suit to Kings and the Kings down in suit to Aces.

Play: Only the cards on the tops of the piles can be moved. First, build them onto the foundations; then build them on each other, one card at a time, either up or down, regardless of suit or color. You can reverse direction on the same pile.

When building, only a Queen can go on a King (or vice versa) and only a deuce can go on an Ace.

When you run out of moves, the deal is over.

Special: In the first deal, you are limited in placing cards on the foundations.

1. Only the cards at the sides of the layout can go on any foundation.

2. The cards at the top may be played only to the Kings line.

3. The cards at the bottom may go only on the Aces line. In redeals (you get two), any card of the right suit and rank can go on any foundation. You're not limited in this odd way.

Redeals: Two. To redeal, gather the piles counter-clockwise, starting in the upper left-hand corner. Then deal the cards, starting at the left-hand corner, as far as they go.

Louis

Other Names: St. Louis, Newport

Level: Moderate.

Play: Exactly the same as *St. Helena*, except:

1. After you deal the first 12 cards of the piles, play everything you can onto the foundations; then fill the spaces from the stockpile. After that, deal the rest of the cards.

2. All cards in the layout can be played to the foundations without any restrictions—in all deals.

3. Building on the layout piles must be in suit.

Box Kite

Play exactly the same as *St. Helena,* except:

1. There is only one deal, with no restrictions on it.

2. Aces can be built on Kings and Kings on Aces.

3. When the top cards of two foundations of the same suit are in sequence, one or more cards may be transferred onto the other foundation. The original Ace and King may not be transferred, however.

Sly Fox

Other Name: Twenty

Space: Moderate.

Level: Easy.

Fate or free will? It's free will in this game of choices!

Layout: Set out four Aces—one of each suit—vertically at the left, and four Kings—one of each suit—vertically at the right. Then deal out four rows of five cards between them. The Aces and Kings are foundations on which you are going to build.

To Win the Game: The Aces need to get built up to Kings, and the Kings down to Aces, by suit.

241

Play: Build on the foundations using the cards in the middle of the layout. As each space opens up, fill it with a card from your hand.

When you can't make any more plays, start going through the cards, one by one. If you can play a card onto a foundation, do so. But if you can't, place it on one of the 20 cards that lie between the foundations. You have your choice of which one. As you place it there, count it (do not count the ones that you put on the foundations, though).

When you have placed 20 cards on the 20 cards that lie between the foundations, stop going through the cards. Now you can make any new plays that have become possible in the layout.

Each time play comes to a standstill, start going through the cards again. But this time, don't fill the spaces with cards from your hand. And as before, after you place 20 more "unplayable" cards onto the layout, stop and make the moves to the foundations that have become possible.

Note: There is no limitation on the number of cards that you may play to any card in the layout. You could play all 20 on one card, if you wanted to. Or, you can be sly, like a fox!

Colorado

Space: Large.

Level: Easy.

Some say this is *Sly Fox* in sheep's clothing. It is very similar to that game.

Layout: Deal two ten-card rows of cards. Above them, you'll set up a foundation row of four Aces and four Kings, as they become available.

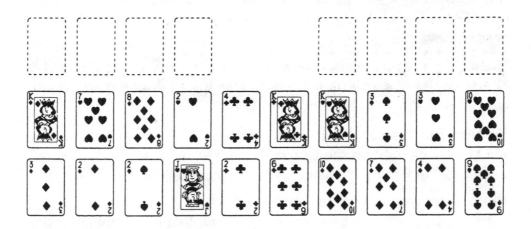

To Win the Game: Build the Aces up to Kings and the Kings down to Aces in suit.

Play: First, play whatever you can to the foundations. As spaces open up in the layout, fill them at once with cards from the stockpile.

When you've made every move you can, start playing one card at a time from your hand. If the card can't go on the foundation, you can put it on top of any card in the layout.

No card can be moved off the layout except to place on a foundation.

Spider

Space: Large.

Level: Difficult.

This game has been called "the king of all solitaires."

Layout: Deal out 54 cards in ten piles as follows: six cards in the first four piles, five in the last six piles. Only the top cards should be face up. These piles are the foundations and the layout at the same time, and all the action takes place on them.

To Win the Game: Build eight sequences in downward order from Kings to Aces right on the layout. Once a sequence is built, it is discarded. So to win the game is to have nothing on the table.

Play: After you lay out the cards, make all the moves you can, building down, regardless of suit. Note, however, that even though you're *permitted* to build regardless of suit, you limit yourself when you do it. You are permitted to move a group of cards as a unit only when they are in suit and in correct rank—so while you would never be able to win the game by making only moves that were in suit, it is certainly better to build in suit, if you have the choice.

When you move an entire pile, leaving a blank space, you may move any available card or group of cards into it. Keep in mind, though, that a King cannot move, except into a blank space. It cannot be placed on an Ace.

When you can't make any more moves, deal ten more cards, one on each pile. And again, make whatever moves you can. Follow this procedure for the entire game, dealing another ten cards whenever you're stuck.

All spaces must be filled before you are allowed to deal another ten cards onto the layout.

After you have put together a complete sequence, you don't have to discard it right away. You may be able to use it to help build other sequences.

The Sultan of Turkey

Other Names: The Sultan, The Harem, Emperor of Germany

Space: Moderate.

Level: Easy.

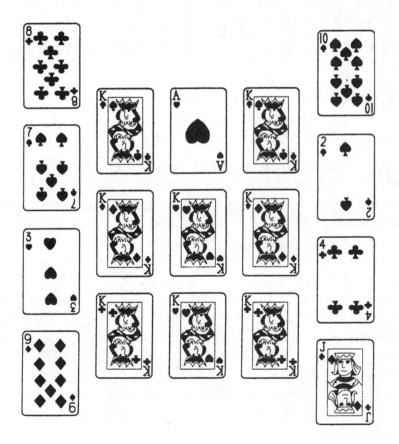

245

Layout: Remove the eight Kings and one Ace of Hearts from the pack and place them as shown in the illustration. Add four cards from the pack on both sides of the Kings. You can use these cards to build onto the foundations.

All the Kings—and the Ace—are foundations, except for the King of Hearts that is in the middle of the square. Don't build on it.

To Win the Game: Build all the Kings (except the middle King of Hearts) up to Queens, in suit—and build the Ace of Hearts to a Queen, also.

Of course, in order to build up the Kings, you're going to need to add an Ace before starting on the deuces.

Play: Go through the cards one by one and start adding to the foundations. Any cards you can't use go into a wastepile.

As soon as a space opens up in the layout, fill it at once, either from the wastepile or from your hand.

Redeals: Two. Shuffle well before going through the cards a second and third time.

The most delightful aspect of this game is the way it looks when you win. Try it.

Tournament

Space: Large.

Level: Easy/Moderate.

Layout: First, deal two columns of four cards each, one to your left, one to your right. These are the "kibitzers." If no Aces or Kings appear among them, put the cards back and deal again.

Next, deal six columns of four overlapping cards each. They are called the "dormitzers."

Then, as they become available, place one Ace and one King of each suit—the foundations—between the kibitzers, as in the illustration on the next page.

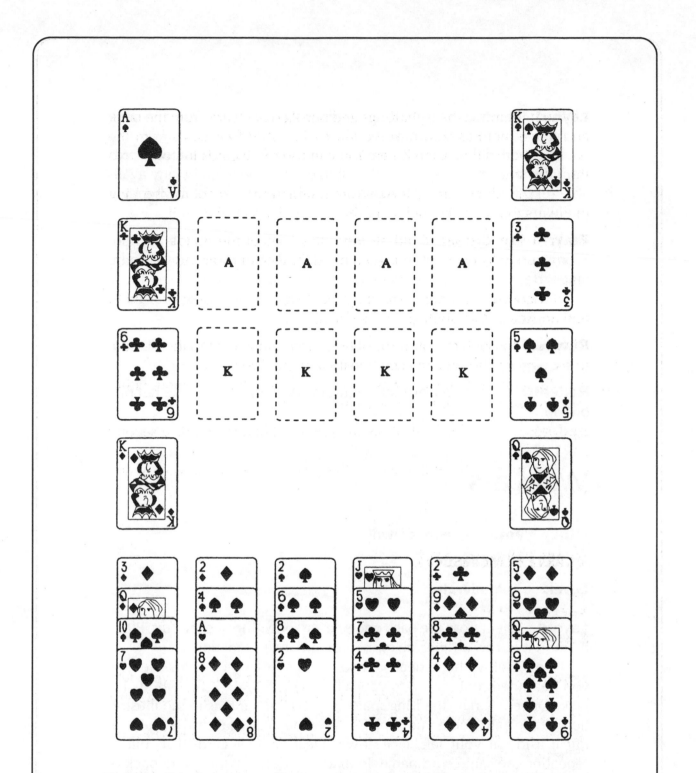

To Win the Game: Build Aces up to Kings and Kings down to Aces in suit.

All the kibitzers and the exposed cards of the dormitzers are available for playing onto the foundations.

A space in the dormitzers must be filled right away with four cards from the stockpile. A space in the kibitzers may be filled by any available (exposed) card from the dormitzers, but you can do it whenever you want.

Play: Make whatever moves you can from the kibitzers and the dormitzers to the foundations. When there are no more moves to be made, deal another four cards to each of the six piles of the dormitzers. If you have less than 24 cards to deal, that's all right—just put them down as far as they will go.

Reversal: When the top cards of two foundations of the same suit are in sequence, one card may be transferred onto the other.

Redeals: Two. To redeal, pick up just the dormitzers, with the last pile on top.

Weavers

Other Name: Leoni's Own

Space: Moderate.

Level: Moderate.

Layout: Select from the pack one Ace and one King of each suit. Place them in two rows, Kings on top. These are the foundations.

Now, below them, deal out two rows of six face-up cards each. As you deal them out, count to yourself, "Ace, 2, 3, 4, 5, 6, 7, 8, 9, 10, Jack, Queen, King" (the King space is off to the right, as in the illustration). If the card you name appears as you name it, that card is an Exile. Put it aside at your left, face down. Deal another card in its place, repeating the same card name. In that way, deal out the entire pack of cards.

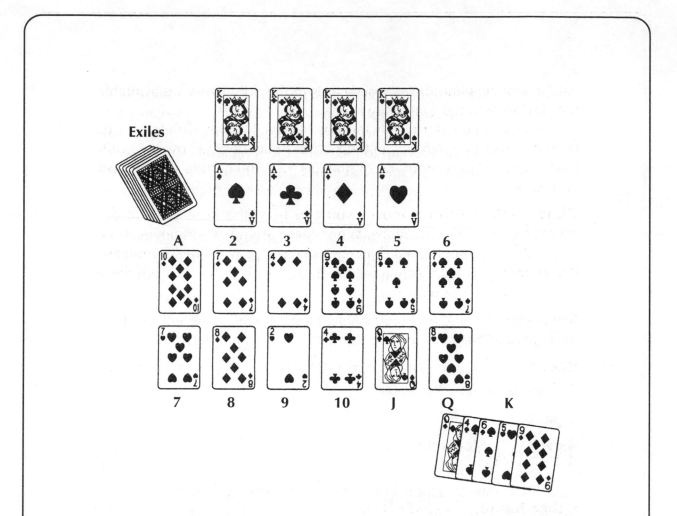

Play: When all the cards are laid out, build what you can to the foundations. All the top cards of the piles are available, plus all the cards in the Kings pile. Spread the Kings pile, so that you can view all the cards at the same time.

Then uncover one card from the cards at your left—the Exiles. If the Exile card can be played onto a foundation, you must play it. If it cannot, place it at the bottom of the pile that corresponds to its number. If it is a 3, for example, slip it under the 3s pile. Then take the top card from the 3s pile—let's say it's a Queen—and slip it under the Queens pile. Continue in this way until you can place something on a foundation. If you turn up a King, however, all play stops.

Slip the King on the bottom of the Kings pile, and turn up the next Exile card.

Reversal: When the Ace foundation and the King foundation of the same suit are in sequence, you are permitted to shift all the cards from one foundation onto the other. Let's say, for instance, that you have built the Ace foundation up to the 6 and the King foundation down to the 7. According to this rule, you could move the 6, 5, 4, 3, and the 2 onto the King foundation. You are not allowed, though, to move the original Ace or King.

Redeals: Two. To redeal, gather the cards up beginning with the Kings pile and go backwards through the cards to the Ace pile, so that Kings are on top, Aces on the bottom.

Windmill

Other Names: Propeller

Space: Moderate.

Level: Moderate.

There's plenty of action in this hypnotic game, and some strategy is useful.

Layout: Put an Ace in the middle of the design, and then deal two more cards in each direction in the shape of a windmill.

Play: Go through the cards in your hand, one by one. As Kings become available, put them in the angles of the windmill, as shown in the illustration by the dotted lines. They are the foundations. You will build down on them, regardless of suit. The central Ace is also a foundation. You will build up on it regardless of suit. Put unplayable cards in a wastepile.

To Win the Game: Build the Kings down to Aces, regardless of suit, and build up the Ace in a continuous sequence (also regardless of suit) until it contains 52 cards—four times through the Ace-to-King sequence.

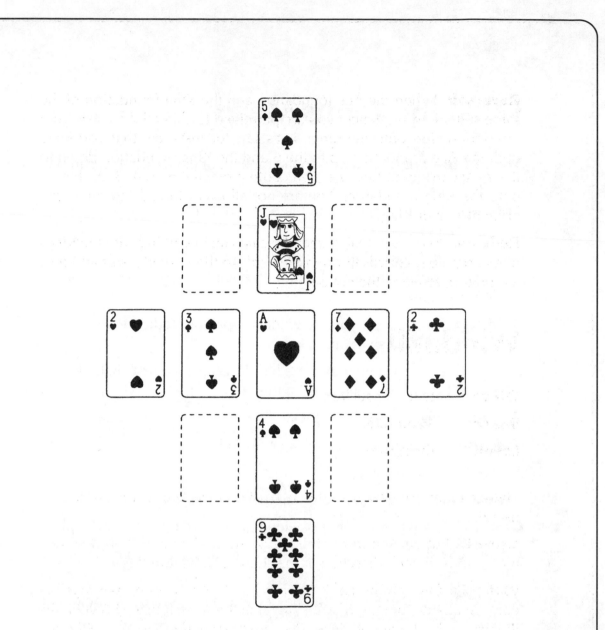

You can use the cards in the windmill shape for foundation building. When a space opens up in the windmill, fill it from the wastepile or, if there is no wastepile, from the cards in your hand.

It is legal to steal the top card from a King foundation to use for the Ace foundation on these conditions: that you use only one card at a time, and that the next card to go on the Ace foundation must come from a regular source.

What the Terms Mean

Around the corner: Refers to the ranking of the cards. Ace can be high and low.

Ante up: To put counters into the pool, so that they may be won during the game.

Base cards: In solitaire, refers to scoring cards, usually but not always Aces, which are built up to complete a set, usually a full 13-card suit.

Bidding: Stating what you are willing to pay or predicting the number of tricks you hope to win.

Book: The basic number of tricks bid. In *Whist*, the first six tricks won. In *Authors*, four cards of the same rank.

Capot: Trying to win all the tricks.

Chicane: A hand without a trump card in it.

Deuce: A 2 of any suit.

Follow suit: Put down a card that matches the suit of the lead.

Gin: To lay down your whole melded hand, face up, ending the play.

Honor card: Ace, King, Queen, Jack of trumps, and sometimes the 10.

Knock: To lay down all melds and declare the face value of unmelded cards.

Lead: The first play that establishes the suit to follow.

Marriage: A meld of King and Queen in the same suit.

Meld: To match up three or four cards of a kind or in sequence. Can be held in hand or put down on the table. A matched set.

Nullo games: Games in which you must avoid taking certain cards.

Picture cards: Jack, Queen or King.

Revoke: Not following suit when you could have and were supposed to.

Spot cards: Any card from 2 to 10.

Suits: There are four: Hearts, Diamonds, Clubs and Spades.

Sweep: In *Casino*, capturing all the cards on the table in one play.

Trick: A sequence of cards in which each person plays a card according to certain rules.

Trump suit: A named suit that can overtake others, chosen in a specific way for each game.

Upcard: The top card of the stock, turned over beside the stockpile, which starts the discard pile.

Widow: An extra hand or number of cards that may be substituted for a player's own hand or held until a certain point in the game. Also, extra cards taken with the first tricks in *Hearts*.

Wild cards: Cards that prior to the game may be given any value you choose.

Index